JOURNEY TOGETHER

DAVID HAWKINS, PhD

HARVEST HOUSE PUBLISHERS
EUGENE, OREGON

Cover design by Connie Gabbert Design + Illustration

Cover Illustration by Connie Gabbert

Interior design by KUHN Design Group

For bulk, special sales, or ministry purchases, please call 1-800-547-8979. Email: Customerservice@hhpbooks.com

This book contains stories in which the author has changed people's names and some details of their situations in order to protect their privacy. This book is not intended to take the place of sound professional medical advice. Neither the author nor the publisher assumes any liability for possible adverse consequences as a result of the information contained herein.

Journey Together
Copyright © 2021 by David Hawkins
Published by Harvest House Publishers
Eugene, Oregon 97408
www.harvesthousepublishers.com

ISBN 978-0-7369-8020-3 (pbk.)
ISBN 978-0-7369-8021-0 (eBook)

Library of Congress Cataloging-in-Publication Data

Names: Hawkins, David, author.
Title: Journey together : turn your marriage into the adventure of a
 lifetime / David Hawkins, PhD.
Description: Eugene, Oregon : Harvest House Publishers, 2021. | Summary:
 "Journey Together will teach you and your spouse to create habits of
 empathy and attentiveness toward each other, ensuring a healthy marriage
 and lasting intimacy"-- Provided by publisher.
Identifiers: LCCN 2020029515 (print) | LCCN 2020029516 (ebook) | ISBN
 9780736980203 (pbk.) | ISBN 9780736980210 (ebook)
Subjects: LCSH: Marriage--Religious aspects--Christianity.
Classification: LCC BV835 .H39 2021 (print) | LCC BV835 (ebook) | DDC
 248.8/44--dc23
LC record available at https://lccn.loc.gov/2020029515
LC ebook record available at https://lccn.loc.gov/2020029516

Printed in the United States of America
20 21 22 23 24 25 26 27 28 29 / BP-SK / 10 9 8 7 6 5 4 3 2 1

CONTENTS

PREPARING FOR THE
LOVE OF A LIFETIME

Love does not obey our expectations;
it obeys our intentions.
LLOYD STROM

This morning my wife, Christie, asked all of us at the breakfast table, "What was the most exotic vacation you took growing up?"

My son and daughter-in-law were there, and smiles broke out on all our faces.

"Car camping at Yellowstone," I said quickly. "It was pretty exotic for a kid."

"Jamaica," Rita told us. "My best friend in junior high invited me to go with her family. We had papaya milkshakes every day."

"Papaya milkshakes?" I asked.

"They were so good."

As we took turns telling about our travels, I imagined sharing the adventure in each location, and hearing about the trips was enjoyable even when a story included a hint of unsettling danger. Colin said he once had to shake out his shoes every morning to check for scorpions.

Whether our experience is something like trying a new flavor of milkshake or finding it necessary to check our shoes for scorpions, traveling stirs us, opening us up to new possibilities. And, yes, new sights, sounds, and experiences often unsettle us, too—but in a healthy way.

Travel Preparations

As we travel through this book together, we'll experience the bumps in the road that come with any travel. We'll encounter crowded intersections, face unexpected dead ends, and make surprising new discoveries. But this book isn't just any kind of travel book. It's about the kind of travel that opens us up to experiencing the love of a lifetime *through learning how to love well.*

Learning how to love well, a journey with no end, may be the best adventure you'll ever take. At first it might be a bit unsettling, but you'll quickly see that tensions and uncertainty are part of the trip no matter how prepared you think you are.

Recently, I approached Christie as she was preparing for our annual trip to Mexico. She was sitting on the floor with her suitcase in front of her, surrounded by everything she wanted to pack.

"How are you?" I asked.

"Stressed."

"Anything I can do to help?"

"Thanks, but no. I just feel like I'm forgetting something. But I'm so ready to get away from the rain."

"Me too," I said, echoing her sentiment.

Although preparations can sometimes be stressful, we always look forward to our trips to Mexico. Each one includes aspects of travel that are both familiar and new. We stay in a town we know and love but then take short trips to places we've never visited.

Part of the joy of travel for all of us who travel is seeing the sights and sounds we know, including welcome familiar faces and the people we love, as well as anticipating new experiences. But we'll also have experiences we didn't anticipate. Perhaps that why it's said travel changes us. I believe that's true, even as we travel through marriage.

Traveling with an Open Mind

As I write now, we're in Mexico, and I just finished a marriage intensive—a several-day stretch of counseling—with a couple who flew here to work with me.

"We love Sayulita," the wife said about our home-base town after their first day here. "The food here is so fresh, and the people are so friendly."

We settled into our work, and it was immediately apparent that this couple would progress quickly. They were open, receptive, flexible, and resilient, and they leaned fully into our task.

"We want to resolve issues and make our marriage work," the husband said. "We've been separated for six weeks, and neither of us like that. We're eager to learn new skills."

And they did. Our sessions went smoothly, largely because of their openness to discover where they had gone wrong and then learn how to make things right. They recognized the old "road map" for their relationship was no longer working and that sticking to their well-worn path would only lead to more disappointment.

"I must admit I came hoping you would change my husband," the wife shared at the end of the third day. "I really thought he was the problem, and I feared you might not see his issues. But coming to a new place and participating in this intensive counseling really opened my eyes to my part in our problems."

Her husband smiled broadly.

"Same for me," he said. "I almost backed out of counseling because I figured we'd be a thousand miles from home and nothing between us would have changed. I'm so glad we came."

The couple thanked me for my help.

"You should thank each other," I said. "I simply helped hold the space for you both to do your work. You each came with different expectations, and even traveled to a foreign country, but you gave yourselves every opportunity to grow."

Traveling with an open mind is what I hope for you as you move through this book. I want you to become fully aware of your experiences in love, the roads you've taken and those you've avoided. I want you to come to a deeper understanding of the ways you've been challenged in your marriage. And I want you to discover opportunities for growth.

As you approach this opportunity to grow your relationship, it's imperative that you open yourself up to new possibilities, challenging how you view the world—especially your world of love.

Good Intentions Aren't Enough

A desire to travel and see new sights and sounds isn't the same as actually traveling. Intending to build a better and stronger marriage isn't the same as putting in the hard work to draw closer to your mate and have a healthy, happy relationship. In other words, good intentions aren't enough.

I intended to study abroad, but it never happened. I intended to travel to several countries I haven't visited, but that, too, has not happened. Good intentions can leave you disappointed if action doesn't follow.

Several months ago I listened to our grandson Caleb play a beautiful composition on the piano. Impressed and deeply inspired, I hugged Caleb and then took a photo of his music book. I immediately ordered it and vowed to learn this piece so I could play it for him.

Now, several months later, I haven't opened that book.

What happened to my intention to learn this minuet? Why haven't I even opened this music book?

You have your own version of this story, right? You've begun certain activities with the best intentions but then stopped. While you were sincere at the start, life got in the way. Old roads, deeply rutted, pulled you in old directions. Or, to be more honest, something else became more important to you. You weren't as dedicated to losing weight, learning that foreign language, taking that college class—or improving your love life—as you thought.

Achieving our best love life takes more than intention. We must vigorously pursue healthy and vibrant love, trying out new behaviors and attitudes.

This book, a guide for this journey of a lifetime, is about the "more" of love. Those wonderful, heady, butterflies-in-your-stomach feelings of love are wonderful *and possible* throughout your marriage, but it takes work to keep experiencing them.

What does it take to achieve this ongoing, inspiring love? As we travel through this book together, you'll learn the importance of a clear road map, free from diversions and dead ends. You'll learn about the importance of fully appreciating self-defeating traits that steer you off course. And you'll learn about the subtle nuances of traveling well with your mate.

In short, this book itself is a road map that, when followed, will lead you to a stable, enduring, loving relationship.

The Road Ahead

What does the road ahead look like for you in your marriage journey?

I still think there's power in intention. I still believe in buying travel guides to far-off countries we'd like to visit. I still believe in buying music books after listening to ten-year-old children play Beethoven, attempting to fuel the desire to play those compositions as well. And I also still believe in good intentions as they pertain to where we want to go with our relationships. But along with good intentions, we must add work.

I smile at romantic comedies and chuckle when two unlikely lovers find their way to each other. So, yes, I believe in love. But I also believe in the work it takes to sustain it. I believe in the work it takes to identify and alter self-defeating, relationship-defeating traits and cultivate relationship-building skills that knit a couple together. I cry when two people in my work risk taking a new route, giving up routines and being truly ready to learn. I'm moved when a couple finds a way to set aside differences to repair their broken relationship.

So let's take the road in this book together and learn new lessons for your marriage. Learning to love well is perhaps the most exciting journey you can ever take. Are you ready for the love life of your dreams? I can help you get there.

1

WHAT'S LOVE GOT TO DO WITH IT?

Preparing for Your Journey

*It's not a lack of love, but a lack of friendship
that makes unhappy marriages.*
FRIEDRICH NIETZSCHE

Eager for a weekend adventure in Mexico, Christie and I asked friends for some ideas.

"Go to Tequila," one friend said, clearly excited for us. "It's not too far away, it's colonial, and it's fun. You'll like it."

Another friend suggested Tequila, too, and then told us about a great place to stay. We checked it all out on a map, made our hotel reservation, and rented a car. We were set.

On Friday afternoon we packed our rental car and plugged the address of our hotel into the GPS. Then we left Sayulita and headed out onto the highway for our weekend adventure.

Along the way, we chatted excitedly about our trip as our GPS gave us directions. Then after driving along the scenic coast for about an hour, the GPS told us to turn right in 500 feet, onto a small, two-lane road.

"This looks like it might be a shortcut to Tequila, over the mountains," I said.

We continued, commenting on the mango farms and the few, sleepy Mexican towns we drove through. Then suddenly the road came to an abrupt dead end.

"What happened?" I asked. "I don't get it. The GPS can't be wrong, can it?"

"Don't know," Christie said. "I'm sure this was the road it told us to take."

"We did something wrong." I looked around for some indication of our error. "Did we miss a turn?"

"I don't know. Let's go back out to the highway and make sure this was the right turn."

We backtracked the ten miles, still searching for some clue about our mistake. We found none. Back on the main highway, we again critically reviewed the GPS directions. Directed to the same route we'd just taken, we decided to take it again.

Now back on the narrow road, we drove slowly so we wouldn't miss anything. But then we came to the same dead end.

"This is crazy," I said. "What are we missing? I can't believe we just followed the GPS to the same dead end."

"It must be wrong," Christie said, clearly exasperated.

"Do we backtrack one more time?" I asked.

"I guess so. I don't know what else to do."

So we turned around and headed back to the main highway again. The ten miles of backtracking seemed to take forever this time. Once there, we triple-checked the GPS directions against our printed map. Then we followed them again, turning down the same narrow road, driving past the same mango orchards and through the same sleepy towns, watching and hoping for our GPS to give us the missed turn.

And for a third time we came to the same dead end.

"Now what?" I asked. "We've just wasted an hour. Maybe we should go back to Sayulita."

"No," Christie said. "It's just time to ignore the GPS and look for another route. We're going a different way."

"A different way? The GPS is telling us *this* is the way."

"The GPS is wrong! It must need updating. We need to try another route."

We pulled over, took a deep breath, and again studied our printed map. We needed a new way, a new plan. Trusting our GPS wasn't working.

There *was* another way. It appeared longer, but it was likely surer.

"Well, we wanted an adventure," I said, grabbing Christie's hand, determined to improve my attitude. "We've got plenty of gas, plenty of time, and we'll have to trust our instincts."

We took the new route, but to do it, we had to let go of our preconceived idea that following the GPS route was the right way and the only way. In the end, the new route, combined with an adventurous spirit, made for a great trip.

What's Love Got to Do with It?

Our trip to Tequila was a bit like the trip you're taking with me in this book. You have a road map/GPS in your brain telling you exactly where to go and how to get there. It's your authority, right? It always takes you to your destination by the best route.

But what if your internal map, like our GPS, needs updating? It may not have all the most current information for navigating your life—especially your love life. What *seems* right may not *be* right. What appears to be the best route may not actually be the best route.

Now go on an adventure with me. Lay aside your inner GPS, your road map to love, in favor of exploring love from new directions.

Your first challenge is to ask yourself, "What's love got to do with it?" This is a critical question we'll look at in this first chapter and then come back to in all the chapters that follow.

We've been taught that romantic love—the heady "stars in your eyes" feeling—is what love is all about. In fact, that feeling is usually the first thing we think about when we think about love. We've been taught that the feeling of love is what holds a relationship together. But is this true?

That's probably what your inner GPS is telling you. We've all been taught that the romantic feeling of love has everything to do with our love life, and that feeling does have a lot to do with it, to be sure. We wouldn't move past the first date if we weren't attracted, both physically and emotionally, to the person we're with. Certainly those feelings give us the impetus to seek an ongoing connection.

But after the initial blast of excitement, there has to be more. When conflicts enter the scene, and they surely will, we need the skills to encourage the attraction to continue. While we must always have starry innocence, the warmth that comes from feeling respected by and respecting our mate sets the foundation for what is to follow.

You *can* have the love life of your dreams, and you *can* feel that special tingle when you see your mate across the room, *but* you must build upon the initial foundation for your relationship.

I find the concept of *building* lacking in so many marriage books. Many of them fail to tell you exactly what it will take to maintain that heady feeling of love. The authors fail to fully discuss cultivating love and eliminating roadblocks to sustaining it. That's what we'll learn in this book.

So building on the foundation of attraction, let's move into exploring some of the thorny issues you'll face in an intimate relationship. I'll arm you with tools so that when the struggles come, and they will, you can face them with hope and confidence.

What else will give you that hope and confidence? Facing reality. Facing the same old road with the same dead ends (illusions) only leads to profound discouragement. You can't sustain a romantic love life working off an outdated map or faulty GPS. You need to discover a better way.

But what is the better way?

A Better Way

I love the feeling of being in love. We've got to have it, or we give up and push away from one another. But it takes more than that feeling to build a marriage.

Again, when thinking about love, most of us do think about a feeling. Perhaps we even have an image in mind. A romantic dinner with a special someone. A weekend away at an exotic destination with someone giving us their undivided attention. We feel cared for, loved, and perhaps as though we're enveloped in a warm, fuzzy cocoon.

And we should hold on to these feelings. But we should hold on to them loosely. Without the skills necessary for building a healthy, long-lasting relationship, the memory of feeling love is only that—a memory.

A love life of our dreams requires understanding why and how we become disappointed in love. What happens to those loving feelings, and how can we recapture them? What are the mistakes we make again and again, and how do we avoid making wrong turns and coming to dead ends? We must evaluate and honestly assess the directions we're following in our love lives and prepare to alter our course as necessary.

Our Road Maps—Accurate or Not?

We've all heard that love is blind. I suggest that, instead, love is naïve. As I said, I'm a believer in the *feeling* of love, but we must build on that feeling for a healthy marriage. We must critically look at the events in our relationship that sour that feeling, look at behaviors that dampen our enthusiasm for love, and look at the issues clouding our vision and creating discouragement. This will require looking critically at our road maps.

Most of us alter our course reluctantly, if at all. Note how many times Christie and I traveled down the same road to the same dead end, sure that the outcome would somehow magically change. But outcomes don't change unless we do.

You arrive at your destination in life only with an accurate road map to follow. But what if your road map includes faulty expectations, erroneous beliefs, distortions in thinking? What if your road map is wrong? Worse, what if your road map is wrong yet you still cling to it?

Christie and I were fortunate that our GPS was absolutely wrong. While it took us three tries to change our minds, we did finally change our course—and with great results. But what if our relational road maps are only partly wrong, as is often the case? What if they're just missing some critical details we need to direct us through specific challenges?

It's been said we'll become hopelessly lost if we follow a compass that's even two degrees off. This is true in our relationships as well: Two degrees off (if not more!) will put us hopelessly off course. Reflect on this for a moment. What if many of the things you do in your marriage put you in the right general direction for your desired outcome, but you're two degrees off—meaning you have certain beliefs, self-defeating behaviors, or traits that steer you off course?

Most of us are at least two degrees off when it comes to love. Most of us are lost. Yet we know only what we know, so we must begin with where we are today. Then if we learn we're two degrees or more off from our desired destination, we need to create a new road map.

I'm mindful that these may not be pleasant words to hear. Most of us want to hear we're doing all the right things we need to be doing. We don't want to hear what we're doing is wrong. I assure you this book is hopeful, and chapter by chapter, we'll learn how to make course corrections to end up where we intended—with a love life worthy of our dreams.

First, we must admit it when we're lost, that we're following a faulty road map, that we need map correcting and course correcting. Staying on our present course won't lead to a healthy, fulfilling love life.

Hard Times—How Did We Get Here?

It's easy to think feelings of love will last or at least prevail when hard times come. But feelings are fickle.

How do we end up so off course? By following the only internal road map we know. We begin our search for love and connection with only a vague sense of direction, right and wrong, good and bad, inherited from our parents and they from theirs.

We think the way we do because we've essentially been programmed to think this way. Our road map, passed down from generation to generation, is largely unexamined. My parents didn't have a clear map to share with me. They knew only what they knew, unaware their map may not have been the right one for me.

Prior to marriage, I knew little about love. I was told I needed to love and be committed to my wife—period. That was the verbal instruction I received. That instruction, however, conflicted with much of what I saw. I watched my dad become exasperated with my mother, slam kitchen cupboards, and storm out of rooms. I watched him fight and then take flight. I don't remember him ever sitting down with my mother, or her with him, to discuss what was happening. I didn't see him apologize or take ownership for his bad behavior. It's no surprise I adopted some of these traits. This became my road map.

Children adopt what they see, so it's no surprise I thought love meant hiding my true feelings, becoming exasperated when things didn't go my way, and then withdrawing into pouting if the situation escalated.

Add to this training the influence of television on my road map. I was raised with a heavy dose of sitcoms, serials, and movies as my models for life. Men were supposed to act a certain way, and women were to act another. Little of it was healthy, and none, as I recall, was based on anything remotely connected to what we have subsequently learned about healthy love.

My road map for love was designed by my upbringing, not fully chosen by me. Adopted but not reviewed. Accepted but not critiqued.

Like me, you probably inherited your road map. And I suspect that, like me, you haven't reviewed your map, questioned what you've been taught, or really inspected what you're doing. Is it any wonder when the map isn't working? Our beliefs need to be questioned, our thinking needs to be inspected, and our maps need to be updated.

Where Do We Want to Go?

If the map of love given us by television and now the internet and social media doesn't show us where we want to go, where *do* we want to go? Rather than talking about the romantic love we hear about in popular love songs, or feel heady about when reading a love poem, or giggle over as we watch a romantic comedy, or engage in a romantic beach read, I'm suggesting a new route.

A healthy marriage relationship is a stable, secure attachment to one person—your lover. This healthy relationship is relatively free from conflict. Problems are resolved and repairs are made quickly. A love relationship is about enjoying another person and being enjoyed. In this relationship, free from excessive conflict and pain, you retain many of those wonderful feelings that brought you together in the first place. Here, you fully appreciate and enjoy the person who lives life with you.

Does this love life appeal to you? It is available to you, but it's likely that you must change course to access it. To find out, you must become clear about where you are and how you got there.

Over the next several chapters, our work takes us through a series of course corrections. In this ongoing journey, you'll learn more about yourself and how you function—both the good and the bad. You'll learn more about your mate, exploring more and more of who this person is. This deepening connection, filled with joy as well as sorrow, will make both you and your spouse better people.

Can this journey include romantic, loving feelings? Absolutely. It must. But you'll add necessary skills to build on those feelings. As you learn to love well, then, you will likely be loved well in return.

Distorted Road Maps and Faulty GPS

Let's back up and consider in more depth how we get off course. Where did we take wrong turns? How has our map been faulty?

As I suggested, your parents modeled a road map for love. It may have been much like mine with many critical issues never discussed. It's been said that *learning is more caught than taught*. Our learning comes from what we see and experience more than from intentional lessons taught by our parents.

Too often, by the time we've reached adulthood and married, we've traveled far from our desired destination of a healthy, robust love life. We've likely learned and practiced many bad behaviors. We've likely been disappointed in love. It's not that our choice of mate was wrong but rather that we were ill-equipped to navigate the challenges of a marriage relationship. It's not that those exciting initial feelings were to be distrusted but rather that we lacked the skills necessary to maintain those wonderful feelings. If both you and your mate are disappointed because of unmet expectations but have lacked the skills to discuss and manage those expectations, you have likely struggled.

Let's consider some of the ways our road maps may have taken us off course.

Living in a closed system: If our parents conveyed *what happens in this family stays in this family*, they endorsed a closed system. In such a system, we don't seek new thinking and learning or review our road map because we've either been firmly told not to or we've not been instructed on the importance of openness. Staying closed is a sure way to stay stuck.

My father's anger issues, for example, were never discussed. We never sought family counseling. We never sought the counsel of a pastor. My grandfather's drinking problems were only vaguely alluded to. My mother's passive-aggression remained in the background of our family life as well. We were a closed family system, following the only map we had.

Living with marriage or family problems *as if they are normal* keeps us stuck and lost, and this attitude creates a barrier to new learning. We never learn to ask others for help or to review our outdated maps with us. We need input from other people for an open, healthy marriage and family system as well as for the new opportunities for growth that stem from that input.

Do you live in a closed marriage or family system? What problematic patterns of behaving have never been reviewed or updated? Are you open to hearing new information about how you're relating to others and how you might improve?

Trusting only ourselves: Related to the concept of a closed system, many people have learned to trust only themselves. This, of course, reinforces their narrow beliefs and stops them from growing. But to grow and change, we need to hear constructive criticism. We need someone who will look at our road map for love and challenge us.

Your mate—a "helpmate"—is a primary source of growth for you. I cannot emphasize enough the power and importance of listening and learning from your spouse. No one knows you like this one other person. Turning a deaf ear to their counsel keeps you terribly stuck. Listening to their wisdom allows you to learn from them, helping you correct your erroneous road map.

Needing to be right: Early on, many of us learned to point blame or dismiss others, insisting we're in the right. Perhaps we saw it modeled, listening to our parents as they squabbled. (We might have even learned that one way to get out of trouble, albeit temporarily, was to blame or dismiss others.)

The need to be right reinforces the faulty belief that our road map is accurate. Filled with pride, we resist any critical feedback. We tell ourselves what we're doing is working when that is anything but true. We focus on the ways our mate is limited in love rather than on how *we* need to change.

Recently, a man I was counseling scolded me for challenging him to grow in his marriage.

"I know what I'm doing," he said. "It's my wife who needs to change. Why are you being so hard on me?"

"Your wife is doing her work," I said, "but I'm not sure you're doing what you need to do."

"You're harder on me than you are on her."

"No," I said, firm. "When I confront your wife, she takes my feedback and applies it to her life. I don't see you doing that."

He squirmed for a few moments, then stared at me.

Can you hear the rigidity in his words and feel his resistance to change? Can you see how his attitude shifts the focus from him to his mate, keeping him completely misguided and off course? Can you imagine the impact this has on his marriage?

"Her work doesn't look exactly like your work because she's working on herself," I continued. "You can't see it, and in fact, it's not your business to know about it. Your job is to focus on the ways you love or don't love and how *you* need to grow."

Many people I work with are resistant to developing new road maps.

Attached to the maps they have, they dismiss my input and the input of others. Their need to be right supersedes the possibility for change. But sometimes we must focus on our work alone and leave our mate's work to them. In doing so, both partners are likely to grow stronger.

Believing feelings don't matter: Another way we get off course is by disregarding our feelings even though they're a primary way we sense something is amiss. Every map has points of orientation, helping us discern north, south, east, and west. Feelings are our internal points of orientation. Distrusting and denying feelings are two sure ways to maintain an outdated road map. Feelings matter. They're an integral aspect of who you are, and they tell you what you need in life.

Our feelings are like sensors sounding alarms. When feeling loneliness, for example, we're alerted to our need for connection. Feelings of sadness alert us to our need for comfort.

It's critical to spend time understanding what you feel and what your feelings are telling you. They will bring you to your truth and help you reorient yourself to the world. They'll help you understand your core values and what must happen for you to obtain what you need. They'll help you correct that two-degree distortion.

Acknowledging your feelings and sharing them with your mate is an important source of connection. For this to happen, though, your relationship must be a safe place where any and every feeling has breathing room.

Weaving a Story Around Our Road Map

As a marriage counselor, I'm sometimes amazed at how attached people are to the road map they're following. Many times I can't seem to offer enough guidance for them to even consider altering their direction. Can you relate? Have you ever been so attached to a certain direction that no matter how much advice you received to the contrary, you were determined to follow your flawed path?

Repeatedly reinforced in our minds, a faulty road map takes on a life of its own. Our direction, believed and justified, becomes firmer and firmer. We rationalize our path, disregarding information that suggests we're on the wrong road, and then we focus on the minuscule bits of information that reinforce our position. We're attached to our road map, and nothing can pull us away from it.

No wonder many of us remain lost in our love life. No wonder our life doesn't work. We're not open to course corrections.

Think again about the previous examples of directions some parents unknowingly give their children: *your system is closed, you can trust only yourself, you're always right, your feelings don't matter.* If you adopt "truths" like these without inspecting and reviewing them, your road map could be even more than two degrees off. Your road map is the story you rehearse and live out, time and again. Can you see how these degree distortions have a profound impact on you over time?

We need to step back and decline to trust everything we've been told and are telling ourselves. We really don't know it all. What we're doing isn't working. If it were, we would have no need for teachers to guide us into a new life. But for teachers to teach, they must have a student, and right now, that student is you. Trusting others to guide you and offer new insights can have a dramatic impact on your life.

Can you see how critical an accurate road map is to your emotional development and a healthy love life? Can you see that the stories you tell yourself influence your road map?

Living with Illusions and Delusions

Scott Peck was one of the first people I recall willing to confront the idea that we don't tell ourselves the truth. This was not a popular notion when he penned the words in his 1978 book, *The Road Less Traveled*, and perhaps it's no more popular now. We've all heard and read much press about the wisdom of trusting ourselves.

Peck writes about how many people would rather live with their own deception than face the pain of changing course. We are capable, he says, of telling ourselves incredible lies so we can cling to the lives we've meticulously created.

How is it possible to be completely lost and at the same time tell ourselves we know where we are and where we're going? The answer has to do with living with illusions and delusions. Faulty road maps are full of the distorted, outdated thinking we believe. Not only do we believe these faulty road maps, but we justify the directions we take.

This deluded thinking leads to further unclear thinking. Remember two-degree distortions. Distorted thinking, rehearsed and reinforced again and again, leads to a faulty road map. This leads to us getting lost relationally and meeting dead ends.

Hannah is typical of many people who come to me for counseling. Now forty-five and newly divorced, she always believed she knew her way. She'd lied to herself for years about her love life, telling herself it wasn't that bad. But it was.

Hannah is a successful real estate broker, known for being savvy and perhaps a bit cutthroat. She's been married twice, both troubled relationships. She's now disillusioned about love, doubting her ability to attract healthy love, and she came to see me to examine her life and consider changing her direction.

"I feel really discouraged," she said. "After my first divorce, I told myself I would be more careful and not make the same mistakes. But my second marriage failed too. I don't think I was the easiest person to live with."

"You can see things now that you couldn't see then?" I asked.

"Oh yes. I'm watching the guys my daughter is dating and the way she treats them, and I see myself. She's making the same mistakes I made, and I'm afraid for her. I'm afraid for me too."

"What have you learned from those experiences?"

"I learned that I have a temper. I'm controlling. I think I drown out my sadness by working all the time. Am I angrier than I think? I have too many moods and pick the wrong kinds of men. Beyond that, I don't have a clue."

"You're thinking about your life, Hannah," I said. "And that's good. The answers will come if you look closely at your life."

"Two failed marriages and some broken relationships after that. There's a trail of hurt behind me and probably ahead of me if I don't stop and figure this out. I don't really know what I'm doing wrong."

Though guarding her emotions, Hannah was clearly—and

understandably—unhappy. She'd been married for twelve years the first time and the second time for seven. She had relationship experience but didn't seem to be learning from it. What were her faulty thinking patterns? What did she need to change? What did she need to do to course correct and become successful in love?

This woman didn't come to counseling until her mid-forties. Why didn't she seek help earlier, in her twenties, thirties, or early forties? The reason isn't surprising. Hannah didn't seek help because she believed she had the correct road map for living and loving. She believed she knew enough to make her own way. She avoided teachers who might have helped her. She made all the mistakes you read about earlier in this chapter—living a closed life, distrusting others, not owning her mistakes, and ignoring her feelings. She believed in her own beliefs, and she was convinced she could figure things out herself.

She was wrong.

Hannah is not alone. She's like others who believed they knew what they were doing. They trusted the roads they chose, refusing to stop and reconsider their direction. They believed the feeling of love was enough to hold a marriage together. As we've said, it isn't. Love is not enough, and we must be open to reviewing our outdated maps and vigorously seeking course corrections. Those struggling to "find love" are often missing critical information along the way.

Getting Our Road Maps Straight

If Hannah is to have a new life filled with life and love, she must change. She can't just keep to her current course and expect her life to be different. It doesn't work that way. If we want our lives to change, we must change.

Specifically, Hannah must critically review her erroneous beliefs—her illusions and delusions—and make changes. She must explore how the beliefs she's lived by and the road map she's used to guide her are wrong. But she will never make those changes as long as she believes she has the right path before her despite her failures.

It's not too late for Hannah. She has the opportunity to change her life as well as offer fresh perspectives for her daughter. She can teach her daughter to question her decisions and direction.

It's not too late for you, either.

Questioning and doubting our road map isn't easy work, but we all must reach a point where we're willing to admit we don't know what we're doing. We must admit that what we're doing isn't working and that we need teachers—possibly several of them.

As the saying goes, if you do what you've always done, you'll get what you've always got. You probably know the corollary to this: If you do what you've always done and expect different results, you're crazy.

Well, you're probably not crazy, but if you're struggling in love, you are no doubt living with illusions and even delusions. Are you ready to take the huge step of admitting your road map is outdated—faulty—and needs revision? Getting our road maps straight means understanding we need help and guidance from those willing to speak into our lives.

Hannah made a critical decision to come to counseling. This is a huge move for someone accustomed to running their own life. It's not easy for anyone to admit they don't know what they need to know. She took a big step in admitting her life wasn't working and that she was responsible for that. Even more critical was her attitude.

"It's not easy for me to be here," she said. "I never ask for help. I'm not even sure I believe in it. But what I'm doing is definitely not working."

She paused and looked at me, then went on.

"But I don't know what I don't know. In my business, consultants come in all the time to tell us what we don't know. I'd like to think I'm open enough to apply the same concept to my personal life and learn from you."

I appreciated Hannah's attitude of humility. She was now teachable and open to new learning. Scripture has much to say about the power of humility. First Peter 5:6 tells us, "Humble yourselves, therefore, under God's mighty hand, that he may lift you up in due time" (1 Peter 5:6). Written just after Peter said God opposes the proud in verse 5, this admonition indicates humility is a powerful tool for growth. Pride, instead, keeps us hopelessly stuck.

Hannah and I considered an appropriate path for her. We agreed that her road map needed updating. We agreed to explore her attitudes and behavior regarding relationships and love.

Love Is Not "Out There"

One of the first critical insights for Hannah was the need for a shift in her attitude. She believed that if she was open to the love "out there," then love would *just happen* for her. But the truth is love is not "out there," and it doesn't just magically happen.

Many people approach love as if it just happens. Why would they think anything different? Love does just happen, right? But while the act of falling in love does happen, sustaining a long-term, loving relationship is anything but a passive process. This was news for Hannah. She had approached her love life as if she had all the tools she needed for love (wrong) and that if she kept doing what she knew to do, her love life would just fall into place (also wrong).

Love, at least alive and dynamic love, doesn't happen spontaneously like we see in the movies. We can't expect love to just come along. And we don't *find* love as much as we *create* love. Then we build on that love, day after day. We work at it just as we work at anything important to us. We focus on it, dedicate ourselves to it, and nurture it.

This was a powerful shift in focus for Hannah.

What Change Requires of Us

The importance of Hannah seeking counseling was not so much that she believed I had all the answers but that she was ready to doubt herself and become a seeker.

Consider that the cost of change requires following this step. Being open to change means accepting the fact that your life will be disrupted with change. When we admit we're lost and going in the wrong direction, we have a sense of instability. *What do I do now? If I'm lost, where am I? Where do I need to go? What changes must I make?*

Change first requires the willingness to admit we're misguided. Directionless. Confused by faulty GPS. *If the direction I'm traveling doesn't bring the results I want, what am I to do?* Can you sense the temporary confusion?

As you approach change, you must also look into parts of yourself that resist the change process. This is a hard truth. We've spent a lot of energy meticulously creating the exact lives we have, so we cling to them even as we also complain about them. That's the truth of the matter. It's true for me, and it's true for you.

I can't count how many people have come to counseling with me, vowing they want to change, only to drop out when the going got tough. Then they no doubt drift back to their previous ways of coping with their problems rather than doing the work to solve them. I anticipate that temptation to quit and even prepare counselees for it so they can steel themselves against it.

Change is difficult. It requires us to admit we've been denying our negative tendencies passed down from generation to generation as well as our tendency to lie to ourselves. It requires us to admit we're stuck and need help.

And so like Hannah, all of us must doubt ourselves. We don't know as much as we think we know. Our relationship GPS could be faulty, and if so, we're likely headed for some dead ends. We've developed patterns of interacting and loving that have led us off course. A bright light must be shed on our behavior and attitudes, and a strong dose of humility must enter our lives, leading us to the change we need.

Being Filled with Love

What is the change we desperately need? We've already discussed how not having a fulfilling love life can result from outdated road maps or faulty GPS. Your work is to doubt yourself and humbly review how you've been living and loving, probably with a skilled teacher or counselor. It's about taking an honest look at how far off your relational map has been.

Remember, a healthy love life is not only about *doing* things differently, as important as that is, but about *being* different. It's about changing from the inside out, not from the outside in. Our actions must match our intentions. It's about being humble and open to learning how we can be healthy, wholesome individuals capable of attracting another healthy, wholesome person into our life. When we are filled with love, we will attract love.

Imagine how people will respond to you if you're filled with hate, fear, or greed. What if you're reactive and angry when things don't go your way? Who will choose to be near you? Probably only someone with similar traits. Imagine inviting a person into your life and then revealing to them how much hurt, pain, and fear you harbor in the secret corners of your life.

Our work in this book is about helping you inspect the secret corners of your life and cleaning them out, then updating your road map and journeying into being more loving.

What's Love Got to Do with It?

As we close this chapter, I ask again, what's love got to do with it? If we're talking about the feeling of love, then something, to be sure. We need the heart palpitations to move forward in a relationship. But these palpitations won't carry us far enough. When our relationship isn't working, then we must have more than that feeling of love so we can navigate. We need a new road map and new directions. We need a course correction.

And for that course correction, we must let go of the false notions of romance we've all seen and experienced. We must face the fact that it takes far more than a feeling to take us to where we want to be: in a stable, connected, life-giving, and loving relationship.

It's time for straight truth about what does and does not make relationships work. Let's find that truth so you can make good choices for your relationship and still have the possibility of the love life of your dreams.

2

CHECK YOUR BAGGAGE

Understanding Your Triggers and Relational Vulnerabilities

Those who cannot remember the past are doomed to repeat it.
GEORGE SANTAYANA

The couple sat in front of me, crestfallen and discouraged, "hoping for a miracle."

I often hear these words from couples, and I take them seriously. Most of them have struggled for years before seeking help, and this couple's not only saying them but flying to Seattle to work with me for three days indicated they knew they were lost. And uncertain how they got lost, they knew they needed new direction.

This was a huge step for them—emotionally, physically, and financially. They were understandably apprehensive and concerned. Above all, they were exhausted. Trying to find our way, time and again yet failing, is tiring. Relying only on what we know to get us further only leads to more dead ends. The results are often discouraging.

Todd and Barbara knew how to physically travel. They had readied themselves for this trip to Seattle by packing their suitcases and making reservations. But they were unable to travel through life together well because their emotional baggage sabotaged their efforts. For years, however, they believed their road map was accurate, that their GPS would take them where they wanted to go if they just tried the same route again and again.

As we learned in chapter 1, asking for help and admitting we're lost is unnerving. And working with me would be unsettling for this couple. It had to be unsettling. Our work would involve unpacking emotional baggage and inspecting what was inside. Few people really want to do work that requires reordering emotional baggage and discarding behaviors no longer useful. Few want to see what they're doing wrong and take the necessary actions to become healthier. Everyone, however, wants relief and loving connection.

As we also learned in chapter 1, taking a new love journey involves looking closely at the map we're using to guide our romantic life. We learned about the importance of being open to change—not just the change we want but possibly the change we don't want—to set us on a new course.

It was time for Todd and Barbara to inspect their road map, note where they had veered from any successful course, and make corrections. This began by checking their emotional baggage, including examining what they believed and how they behaved and then exploring blind spots so they could change.

Heavy Baggage

Todd and Barbara were typical of so many couples who work with me. Feeling the weight of letdown after letdown because of flawed directions and emotional baggage sabotaging their efforts, they wanted relief.

I reminded them that coming to Seattle was an act of hope. Asking for help is always a strong move, indicating an ability to doubt oneself and reach out to others who might offer insight into our journey. After all, if everything was working in their marriage, they wouldn't need to change course or reflect on their baggage.

"Let's start at the beginning, folks. What has happened to bring you here? You've made a great effort to get here, and that suggests you have some hope. It also suggests that you recognize what you're doing isn't working."

"I don't know how much more I can take," Barbara said, angry. "I keep discovering more and more about Todd, but when I question him, he tells me that's it, the whole truth."

"Please share more," I said.

"Todd has been hiding things. He's never honest, and I have to drag the truth out of him. It's exhausting."

"I shouldn't have to answer to you for everything," Todd said. "You're not my mother. I can't keep getting hammered with what I've done wrong. There has got to be an end to it."

"There would be if you just stopped lying," Barbara said, countering his complaint. "I don't trust you."

I interrupted them. We wouldn't get anywhere with each one shouting accusations at the other, which they had likely been doing for some time.

"Do you want to tell him everything, Todd?" Barbara asked, glaring at him with disgust.

Todd gritted his teeth and seemed defiant. A confident businessman, he wasn't familiar with answering for his actions. He struggled to sit with his wife's anger and frustration with him over his avoidance, denial, and deception. I sensed him beginning to withdraw in the face of her anger.

"The more I try to dig myself out of this hole, the deeper it gets. She's not going to believe anything I say."

"Try me," Barbara said abruptly. "Try telling the truth so I don't have to ask ten thousand questions and play private detective. I'm so tired of this. I'm exhausted. Just tell the truth."

Barbara wiped tears from her eyes, looking to me for help.

"Can you see how it goes?" she said. "This is killing me, and he seems to think a few simple answers will end this crisis. It's so much deeper than that."

"I hid some money from her," he said softly. "I spent money on gambling, and I like fancy cars, clothes."

He paused, looking at his wife, who was now staring at him.

"And…" she said.

"I don't know what else."

"You've spent money at strip clubs and massage parlors and on online chatting with women, and I keep discovering more. Pornography. Lies. I'm just sick from it all. I can't take it."

And so it went for the next hour. Barbara acted as a prosecuting attorney while Todd downplayed and distorted his actions. I watched as she became more exasperated and he minimized the truth of what he'd done. She ridiculed him as he inwardly bristled, dodging questions in a vain effort to protect himself. They continued spiraling downward as I considered intervention strategies.

"This is obviously very complex, folks," I finally said. "It will take time to unravel it all, but we can do it. Are you willing to critically look at how you've been relating to each other so you can make different decisions going forward? You'll both need to make changes, but they will improve your marriage. To get to the bottom of any of this, you must be prepared to unpack your emotional baggage. We all have patterns of behavior, the roots of which lie deep inside, often from childhood."

My first task was to help them see that their current crisis was but an episode in a much larger drama. Their story had layers, as is the case for every couple, with problems beginning years before this current crisis.

Todd and Barbara needed depth work, as most couples in trouble do. They had this current crisis to navigate, but they didn't get where they were because of this one incident. They had deeper problems with a long history. They would need to make sense of how this current crisis fit with their longstanding patterns that needed attention.

Where had they initially gone wrong? How was their road map wrong? What were the dysfunctional patterns set in place long ago? That was our work to discover.

Two Degrees Off

It's easy to get lost. It's easier still to remain lost. Being lost, or rigidly remaining on our current course, stops us from fully exploring our issues and the impact they have on our marriage. We must stop to reflect on where we've been, on where we're going, and on the emotional baggage we're taking with us.

We're all foolish people in some ways, waiting too long before going to the dentist, doctor, or auto mechanic. This is also true when it comes to seeing a marriage counselor. We get lost in our marriage and stay lost, reluctant to ask for directions even when it's clear (or could be clear) we don't know where we're going. Stubborn pride stops us from asking for help.

Remember what I said happens when, over time, we continue on a route that's two degrees off and yet cling to it? Before long—slowly, perhaps—we inevitably become lost. We just don't know we're lost because the mistakes can be subtle and because denial is powerful.

Most of you have heard the story of the frog in the kettle. It's worth retelling.

If you put a frog in a kettle of boiling water, it will do all it can to get out. But if you put it in a cool pot of water and heat the water incrementally, say two degrees at a time, the frog will stay in the pot until it dies.

While Todd's current behavior caught Barbara off guard in some ways, in other ways she wasn't truly surprised. She'd known something was wrong in their marriage.

"Todd has always been secretive," she said, now reflecting on the past. "This is simply the latest in a series of longstanding problems. When I'm really honest with myself, I must admit I've seen problems from the beginning. I ignored them, and now I'm paying the price."

What a bold admission. When Barbara is honest with herself, she, like all of us, admits deeper problems exist. She's been in as much denial as Todd has, though hers has looked a bit different from his. She knows their issues didn't just begin, and she knows she's enabled them to continue. While she's been taken off guard by the current crisis, it's not a crisis that arose out of nowhere. Rather, she's been like the frog in a pot of water, content to sit while the temperature slowly and dangerously rose.

How I wish we could all be honest with ourselves about the water temperature rising in our marriages. How I wish we could make a habit of inspecting our emotional baggage, paying close attention to patterns of behavior that might have had a purpose early in life but aren't helpful now.

Bricks in Their Bags

Todd and Barbara have been traveling for a long, long time at least two degrees off and weighed down by emotional bricks in their bags. Picture traveling with bricks in your backpack. Over time, any extra weight, even ounces, becomes burdensome. Such is the nature of the self-defeating patterns of behavior we will be exploring.

Off course and weighed down is a terrible combination. Todd and Barbara had longstanding issues. Their current crisis was only the latest in a series of disappointing discoveries for Barbara.

"When I look back, I remember finding receipts I couldn't explain," she said. "I remember asking him about missing money, and he always had explanations. I'd see pornography on our computer, but he'd deny knowing anything about it. I feel like such a fool now."

I've grown accustomed to people's resistance to facing issues. I know the human tendency is to deal only with the crisis at hand while avoiding all the underlying issues—packing away emotional baggage.

Unpacking the Baggage

We can't change what we don't own, and we can't own what we can't see and understand. This is the task of unpacking our emotional baggage.

"I'm just now putting all the pieces together," Barbara said. "I'm sitting back and seeing the whole pattern. Looking at one issue, close up, makes it easier to deny the severity and longstanding nature of the situation."

"You've been married over thirty years," I said. "Do you believe the problems go back to the start of your marriage?"

Todd jumped in.

"Look. We have a lovely home, nice cars, and two beautiful, grown children who went to good colleges because of my work. If I was some kind of criminal, we wouldn't be living the lifestyle we're living."

Clearly feeling threatened, Todd was still trying to deflect and minimize their problems. As I tried to explore his baggage, he shifted the focus away from himself, continuing to brag about their lifestyle.

"Certainly, you've done some things well, Todd," I said. "That's not the question here. What we want to do is take a thorough inventory of the problems you've hidden in the shadows so they don't recur and so you and Barbara can heal."

Todd was agitated, a signal that he was afraid of feeling even more hurt or shamed.

"We just want to understand the bigger picture, Todd," I said. "You're not a bad person, and you haven't set out to hurt Barbara."

"Nothing like this is going to happen again," he snapped, seeming not to have felt reassured. "I've learned my lesson. I know if I do anything like it again, she'll divorce me."

"You certainly mean well when you say that," I said. "Your hands have touched a hot stove that you won't soon touch again. But in time, you'll forget the pain of the hot stove, and who knows what might happen?"

"Exactly," Barbara said, again looking at Todd.

I shared with them that relapse into any problematic behavior often occurs because the possibility of relapse isn't taken seriously. That's what was occurring now with Todd, and it's what gets most couples into trouble—the failure to fully explore the depth of their problems and heal them.

"Folks, these problems have been developing for years," I said. "We must look into the emotional baggage of your lives and marriage, the heavy bricks you carry around, to ensure problems are really being explored and healed. Only then can you have any assurance that the problems won't repeat themselves."

Holding the Wound Open

Getting lost doesn't happen in one move. Getting lost, *and staying lost*, takes making the same mistakes again and again and then rigidly staying attached to that route. Staying lost is a failure to make course corrections.

Todd wanted to believe their problems were superficial and that a little help would solve them. But Barbara was wiser now and in much more pain. She was not about to settle for simple solutions. She wanted to fully explore their problems, feel safe, and heal underlying issues. If they didn't heal those issues, Todd would have to attend to her feelings of insecurity and concern again and again.

Doctors know infection is likely to occur if a wound is closed prematurely. It needs to breathe, making it possible to flush out contaminants and heal from the inside out. Such is also the nature of an emotional and relational wound. It must be held open for a time, and doing so takes great dedication. As tempting as it is to rush the healing, suturing an emotional and relational wound closed too quickly leads to greater problems.

What if instead of impatiently rushing forward, Todd were to say to Barbara, "I know you've been hurt deeply. I've lied to you and broken your trust. I'm really sorry. I know you need to talk about all this and ask questions. I'm willing to listen non-defensively for as long as it takes."

Rather than Barbara carrying the burden of holding the wound open alone, imagine her relief if Todd carried that responsibility as well. Imagine if she didn't have to force him to sit with her to explore the depth of their problems. This is a most powerful step for couples trying to heal.

The Power of Denial

Holding a wound open means staring into the face of denial, sorting through emotional baggage. It means dedication to discovering truth, no matter how painful, knowing that by doing so we can discover true healing.

This is hard work, requiring you to doubt yourself. It means recognizing that just as surely as you want to get to the bottom of what's causing your problem, part of your personality stands guard, ensuring secrets remain secret. There is a real threat, after all. Secrets often carry shame, and it can be hard to sit with that. Few people are willing to be fully open and transparent, and so they leave old, destructive patterns intact.

At one point in the session, Barbara began to backpedal, her own denial coming to the foreground. She saw Todd bristle and perhaps became fearful.

"He's not all bad," she said. "Maybe I'm being too hard on him. He can be charming, and he's been an excellent provider. He loves me and our two children. He's a hard worker and a leader in his company, at our church, and in our community."

Like a mosaic is filled with varying pieces, life is filled with both joys and sorrows. It's easy to overlook problems, hoping and wishing they will just disappear. We all tend to embrace this denial, this magical thinking

Denial is powerful. D.E.N.I.A.L means [I] Don't Even Notice I Am Lying [to myself].

Like for the frog, the water holding Todd and Barbara's marriage was fine in the beginning. But then, long ago and slowly, it started to heat amid their building a family, starting careers, and just living life. Todd's issues with deception, financial unfaithfulness, pornography, and sexual infidelity had been part of his personality and their marriage from the beginning. But now both he and Barbara were using denial to tell themselves matters weren't as severe as they actually were.

While Todd and Barbara's story may not be your story, we're all challenged when it comes to facing our problems. None of us want to look our problems square on. We want to believe denying them will magically make them go away. Living with the weight of our emotional baggage seems somehow better than facing the truth. We feel the weight of the bricks, but nonetheless, we deny their existence.

Denial perpetuates problems, and it's the primary reason so many marriages end up in catastrophic trouble. The problems have always been there lurking below the surface, yet they were ignored.

Scripture implores us with this advice: "The simple believe anything, but the prudent give thought to their steps" (Proverbs 14:15). Giving thought to our steps means being honestly reflective. But few people are willing to give complete thought to their steps and check their emotional baggage. Few are willing to be dedicated to the truth no matter the discomfort. This is the power of denial—lying to ourselves about the severity of the problem.

The Benefit of Denial

In a strange way, our denial protects us, and we cling to it. We deny and avoid problems and then develop even greater, unhealthy coping patterns to manage them.

Todd had used denial to cope during childhood when his parents, both alcoholics, fought and struggled in their own lives. He learned to compartmentalize his pain, excelling in sports and academics. Then into adulthood, he blocked out his emotional pain, focusing on the aspects of his life that brought relief, using addictions to cope with his inner emotional pain.

Todd became secretive and entitled—he lived with a *closed system*. He believed he knew all he needed to know and that he didn't need to rely on others. He never faced his emotional and relational problems, and he certainly didn't reach out for help.

Todd worked hard and justified giving himself whatever he wanted. His parents didn't seem to care about him when he was young, and then he determined to give himself whatever he wanted, becoming impulsive and demanding. When marital problems surfaced, as they do for everyone, he believed he was entitled to immediate relief, no matter what form that would take.

While denying his problems and emotional baggage helped him in younger years, it was now causing untold problems in his marriage.

Such are the precursors to much of our denial. Our current problems can often be seen as outdated solutions to problems of days gone by. We must face our denial—fighting against our outdated road map or broken GPS and the bricks we carry in our emotional baggage—if we are to grow.

No One Automatically
Knows Their Shadow Side

Facing our denial means getting to know our shadow, where those aspects of our personality we lie about to ourselves reside. I don't mean just acknowledging our shadow but becoming really familiar with it.

Few of us take the time to know our shadow side, the emotional baggage we bring into every relationship. We don't explore our self-defeating traits and how we got them. We would rather focus on what we do well, the bright places in our personality.

A few rare individuals spend a lifetime in psychotherapy and reading, praying, and retreating in a dedicated effort to understand their shadow side. By and large, though, most refuse to do this rigorous, painful work.

Why do most people refuse to inspect what lurks in the shadow side of their personality? Who wants to admit those less than admirable traits? Who wants to stare directly at the parts of themselves that are immature, self-centered, and perhaps even manipulative and willing to take advantage of others? To fully know our shadow side would require us to work on those parts.

Studies show we're much more likely to evaluate our own actions in a favorable light while critically reviewing the actions of others. We self-righteously judge the actions and motives of others while letting ourselves off the hook.

My life is an example.

I went through most of my young adulthood angry with my father. I viewed his disciplinary style while I was growing up as tyrannical and his staunch work ethic as overly focused. I often thought he was excessively religious and narrow-minded. As I matured, however, I began to see his life in broader terms. I began to appreciate how hard he worked for our family of seven. Additionally, I began to see how much like him I had become. My questions shifted from *What kind of father was he?* to *What kind of son was I?* and *What kind of father and husband have I become?* This has been "shadow work" for me.

Seeing my father in more gracious terms while also seeing myself more realistically has benefited me greatly. Seeing others more graciously and inspecting ourselves more rigorously can be very beneficial.

If You Spot It, You Got It

No shortcuts to checking our baggage in the shadow of our personality exist. If we don't want our shadow Self to sabotage our marriage and other relationships, however, we all must do it. One way to do this work is through observing how frequently and in what ways we criticize others.

Perhaps you've heard the phrase "If you spot it, you got it." This means whatever we criticize in others is a trait we likely have in ourselves. We're able to see it because we have the same trait within ourselves, and thus we're sensitive to it.

This is a harsh truth, to be sure, but it's a powerful way to peer into our shadow Self. I don't want to admit having traits like those I criticize. I would much rather believe I'm free from detestable traits, projecting them onto others instead.

"It's not me," I whisper to myself, hoping to sell myself on this belief. Facing our shadow side is hard work, and it can be quite frightening. What will we discover there? Are we more self-centered than we want to believe? Are we more demanding and controlling than we think we are? Are the behaviors we see and detest actually hidden parts of ourselves clamoring for attention?

If you spot it, you got it. In other words, whatever troubles you about someone else is likely something you also disdain within your own personality. Whether or not this is wholly true, an exercise like this is most useful, especially in your marriage: When feeling impatient toward your spouse, ask yourself if you, too, are at times impatient. When you feel threatened by your mate's actions, ask yourself if you, too, can be threatening with yours. When the person you married is pushing you away, ask yourself when you're inclined to push someone away.

Bristling Hints at Our Shadow Side

Another sure path to discovering what lurks in our shadow side and the bricks we carry in our emotional baggage is noting what makes us bristle. When someone, such as your mate, causes you to bristle, look at your reaction a bit closer.

While it's tempting under such circumstances to point a finger of blame at your mate, consider the possibility that they have simply exposed a raw spot likely there long before aggravating it. With the aggravation comes the possibility of doing inner work and healing this wound yourself—or at least lessening its impact.

Richard Schwartz, author of *You Are the One You've Been Waiting For,* says this: "It's always difficult to get each person to go inside toward their own pain rather than attack the perceived source of it in their partner...We can use any difficulty in life that produces an extreme reaction as a path to parts we need to heal."[1]

The next time you bristle, pause and listen to what your body is saying. Instead of maintaining your focus on what your mate has done that annoys you, look inward. Why are you bristling? Examine what's there with loving compassion.

The Breakdown That Leads to the Breakthrough

Being cracked open by a crisis is an opportunity to check our baggage. Denial works for only so long, and we can keep our baggage in the shadows for only so long. We can travel only so far being two degrees off before we become lost and trouble happens.

But the window of opportunity for Todd and Barbara to address their deeper problems is brief if they give in to denial, if they decide to stick with their life as it is as long as it works for them again in some fashion.

But with this crisis, if they can see it as a moment of truth, they have the opportunity to update their faulty GPS and develop a healthy love life. If, however, they settle for quick, simplistic solutions, they'll just face another crisis in the days ahead.

To get to the heart of the trouble in their marriage, both Todd and Barbara must allow themselves to fully experience "the breakdown that leads to the breakthrough." In other words, they must admit that their lives have fallen apart, then consider a new way of doing things, a new path to travel. Their emotional baggage must be dumped out before them so they can see what's there.

Some time ago—and I'll talk more about this later—I faced a particularly difficult period in my marriage. Christie called a sudden and challenging halt to my selfishness. She emotionally and physically pulled away to consider our marriage and give me an opportunity to look at myself.

I must admit that I first faced her actions with anger, soon followed by fear and discouragement. But I was counseled to soak in this time apart, to allow it to work on me rather than me trying to work on it. I was encouraged to think, reflect, pray—but *not* to act. I was encouraged to see this time as a gift, a chance to decide what I truly wanted. I was encouraged to *see* what was exposed in this crisis.

This was a most challenging task. Seeing a crisis as a gift is no easy endeavor. My denial kicked in quickly. At first I viewed myself as a victim, seeing her action as excessive. Gradually, however, I settled into a thoughtful time. Scripture tells us to rejoice in good times and to consider in bad times (Ecclesiastes 7:14). This is sound counsel.

Without a breakdown in our customary way of doing things, there can be no breakthrough. Anytime we try to short-circuit the process, we cheat ourselves. We must become lost before we'll take a different route. We must be burdened by our heavy emotional baggage before we open the suitcase and thoroughly examine what's there.

Intervention

Sometimes our breakdown occurs at the hands of an employer. Sometimes it happens with a friend. At other times, as with Todd, the breakdown occurs because of an angry spouse. In whatever way it might occur, a crisis that leads to an intervention is an opportunity not to be squandered.

Interventions—ultimatums where change must occur or else something worse will happen—are typically times of intentional interruption in the dailiness of life. Listen to Barbara's words:

"I will not go forward now. We must get to the bottom of what is going on. I don't care about the cost or what it takes. I'm not going to use Band-Aids any longer to try to patch things together. We have to get to the root of the problem and find solutions that will work for us going forward."

Todd was understandably threatened. Barbara was taking a stand. Change, one way or another, was going to happen. He faced a critical moment in his life and marriage.

"You're not going to quit until you find what you're looking for, even if it's not there," he told his wife with a sharp tone.

His denial remained strong as I watched him cling to his old life. Todd was showing his distorted thinking again as he attempted to blame Barbara for their difficulties. Barbara, however, would not be deterred. It was time for an intervention. She was ready for radical change.

"The road stops here, Todd," she said. "If you want to stay married to me, and I hope you do, we have to fix what's broken. You must trust that I have our welfare in mind. I'm for you, and I'm for us."

In this case, as is often the case, one person is driving the intervention. Barbara is no longer interested in enabling their marriage to stay the same. She knows simple answers won't work. As with any kind of severe, ongoing problem, someone must shout, "This must stop. Enough!"

Resistance

Change never occurs easily. Change is disruptive. And when one person in a relationship is prepared to intervene and seek change, the other often resists it. One is willing to look into the shadows, exploring what's hidden in the baggage, while the other seems only willing to continue in denial.

This is not surprising and must be expected. Resistance to change is universal and must be anticipated. One party wants change, growth, and healing while the other pushes back, clinging to their old way of life. Yet the resistance must not hinder the courageous one from forging ahead, shining a light into the shadows.

Dr. Henry Cloud, in his book *Changes That Heal*, helps us understand how someone can become lost, attached to their distorted world. He reminds us that "the law of entropy holds that any system left to itself becomes more and more disordered over time. This is what happens in emotional isolation. As people are shut off from others, their anger, sadness, and depression begin to interfere with their thinking processes. Their circuits overload, and their thought processes become distorted."[2]

Certainly Todd had become isolated, his thinking distorted as he lived his life relying solely on his own limited insights. And Barbara had enabled him to continue in that denial by enduring his anger and strong resistance to change. Now he was resisting her insistence on facing the truth. But her efforts to help him take responsibility for his problems were met with reverse blame and other deflecting tactics.

"He scolds and ridicules me for asking so many questions," she said. "He makes me feel crazy. He could make this so much easier. His anger and intimidation are not new to me, but it has come out more forcefully during this crisis."

Barbara's journey had not been an easy one. I could sense she was preparing herself not only for her own inner change process, including dealing with her resistance to looking at her shadow side, but for continued resistance from Todd as well. She faced the fact that she had enabled this destructive process as she and Todd reinforced each other's denial. But change requires at least one of the partners to insist on change—ideally both.

Taking Responsibility

Our final tool for checking your baggage—and central to healing issues in a marriage—is the practice of taking responsibility. In *The*

Road Less Traveled, Scott Peck speaks clearly on this topic: "We cannot solve life's problems except by solving them. This statement may seem idiotically tautological or self-evident, yet it is seemingly beyond the comprehension of much of the human race. This is because we must accept responsibility for a problem before we can solve it."[3]

Checking our baggage means facing reality. We must courageously look at what is evident before us, but we must also peer into our shadow side to find those self-defeating traits that repeatedly sabotage our relationships.

Taking responsibility for our emotions and actions is never easy work, but it's also incredibly rewarding. It's the only path to ending ongoing conflict in our marriage—and in other relationships—and finding true healing. Taking responsibility is a powerful concept and activity as we courageously face the weight of our actions.

As Todd and Barbara's marriage intensive unfolded in the weeks that followed, Todd gradually came to face truth and the darkness in his life. He admitted to Barbara that he had, indeed, visited massage parlors on a number of occasions. He had gone to strip clubs and chatted with women online. He had lied about these activities and some financial dealings. But now he was able to speak about his intense guilt and shame, bringing moments of relief to his own inner emotional pain. As he faced the truth of his actions, he became more equipped to explore his motivations for them.

Facing the depth of his shameful actions presented an opportunity for change. As long as we lie to ourselves, there can be no real growth. But fortunately, Todd began to face the fact that it was time for change. He was sick and tired of carrying the baggage of his lies and deceitful behavior. He was beginning to be ready for the change he so desperately needed.

Facing truth is like that. We become open to new possibilities, no longer blindly clinging to our outmoded ways of functioning. We admit our lives aren't really working. We open up ourselves and others to the possibility of living an authentic, honest life. Armed with this truth, we can change direction, and this new direction feels right. We can trust this new direction, choosing to course correct as well as empty the heavy bricks out of our emotional baggage. The various parts of us, now fully open to the light, make sense and become coherent.

Todd gradually faced the pain he'd been masking with his acting out. He began to trust Barbara to care for him and his shadow side. He was able to dig deep and root out the pain of his childhood as well as the loneliness and estrangement he felt as an adult, bringing greater compassion from Barbara in the process. For all of us, vulnerability evokes compassion and care from others.

Making Friends with Your Shadow Side

There is no alternative path to the healthy life we want other than facing our shadow side, for that is where we pack the bricks that weigh on us. Rather than hide from our shadow side, we must take out the suitcase of shadowy character traits and inspect what emotional baggage is there. Only by inspecting these outdated attitudes and behaviors can we grow.

The wisdom of Alcoholics Anonymous exclaims, "When wrong, promptly admit it." Indeed, this is the only way to go forward. We must share our stories with others. We all make mistakes, engaging in actions that hurt both other people and ourselves. Not only must we promptly admit wrongdoing, but we must look into the roots and history of that wrongdoing. Why have we lied? Why did we act so selfishly? Why did we take advantage of others for our own gain? Why?

As we make this emotional inspection of our shadow side, we find wounded parts of ourselves that need attention and healing. And we can be compassionate to ourselves as we search the shadows of our personality. While we must take responsibility for our actions, we can do so gently. We weren't trying to be hurtful when we hurt someone. We weren't intentionally wreaking havoc.

Going forward, we must continue the task of making friends with our shadow side. We must compassionately search there for understanding on an ongoing basis. We must seek answers to the tough questions that give our stories meaning. Exploring ourselves with gentleness leads to treating others—and especially our mates—with greater gentleness as well. They, too, are not trying to hurt us. They just have their shadow sides as well.

Ongoing Baggage Inspection

It's not enough to inspect our baggage only once. Our shadow side is too complicated for that. Becoming healthy relationally requires reviewing our baggage periodically. The intervention that stems from a breakdown that leads to a breakthrough is often short-lived, and so we must keep our baggage cleaned out to be prepared.

Someone said we are either recovering or relapsing; there is no middle ground. That means we're either growing, becoming healthier and healthier, or we're succumbing to the powers of denial, becoming more and more lost.

Here are some sobering questions: Where are you in your personal life and marriage? Are you clear about the changes you need to make?

It's critical to weave growth into your life and marriage. Here are some steps you can take to ensure you're growing:

1. *Assume that some aspects to your functioning exist outside your awareness.* We can never be fully aware of our motives and actions. Assume old behaviors and attitudes will rear their heads again.

2. *Remember, if you spot it, you got it.* Whatever bothers you about others is likely important for you to see in yourself. The problems in your life and marriage are not all "out there"; rather, many of them—if not most—are "in here."

3. *See raw spots between you and others as opportunities for healing.* Consider whatever bothers you about someone else—especially your mate—an opportunity for self-understanding and to unload some of the bricks weighing you down.

4. *Continue intentional growth through prayer, reading, support groups, and possibly therapy.* Build growth processes into

your life that mitigate the havoc your shadow side can cause.

And So, What About Love?

The feeling of love is powerful for making the initial connection to another person, but it's less important as the relationship deepens. Actions of love are more important in creating a lasting quality to our relationships.

Actions of love mean having the courage to admit weaknesses. To face the damage we've done and still continue to produce. To refuse to shrink away from facing the grief we cause others. Change comes from doing this hard work.

Embracing love means acknowledging that for our marriage to work, we must rid ourselves of old, archaic attitudes and destructive behaviors. We must explore and own the depths of our actions and replace hurtful behavior with helpful, healing actions.

So this is what love has to do with it. Love means growing up and facing your shadow side. Love means sorting through baggage, holding on to only what is good and throwing out what no longer serves you. You can do this work, and the results will amaze you.

Now let's move forward again, this time exploring the power of being a healthy traveling companion for our mate.

3

TRAVELING COMPANIONS

Choosing to Travel Together, Again and Again

I have found out that there ain't no surer way to find out
whether you like people or hate them than to travel with them.

MARK TWAIN

love traveling—mostly. Christie and I have traveled to several foreign countries, and we have many wonderful and zany stories to tell about our experiences.

We once booked passage on a cruise ship to the coast of Greece after a travel agent assured us it would be the trip of a lifetime. We were shown photos of white hotels tucked neatly into rocky hillsides with expansive views above the Mediterranean Sea.

What we got was a cramped room with bunk beds deep in the bowels of a freighter and a hotel room near the end of an airport runway— no water in sight.

Still, Christie made the best of this experience. Me, not so much. We discovered I'm the more persnickety traveler. I like predictability, a desire we must all hold loosely if we're to enjoy our adventures. I prefer comfortable beds, few surprises, and meals I both recognize and enjoy. Christie is more adventuresome and willing to try new places, foods, and experiences.

I like to get to airports more than two hours before my flight, and I get cranky if we're instead pressed for time. While I don't like to be caught unaware, I still pack the night before or the morning of a trip. If I forget something crucial, I'll buy a replacement somewhere. Christie, though, likes to make lists, packing much more methodically and rarely forgetting anything. (That's why she was stressed while packing for our trip to Mexico earlier in this book; she thought she might be forgetting something.)

After arriving at the airport, I'm relaxed, and I want to chat. Christie prefers to sit quietly and read. I tend to bug her with my excitement.

Based upon our travel IQ, we're incompatible. Fortunately, we've worked through most of our idiosyncrasies and enjoy traveling together. At least I enjoy traveling with her. But traveling has, I believe, helped us grow closer as a couple, though not without some challenges.

Traveling Reveals Issues

Yet, as Mark Twain indicated in the quote at the beginning of this chapter—and whether we're talking about a vacation or how we travel through life—traveling tends to highlight compatibility. Traveling has a way of exposing our character issues, and they're likely to become even more critical to address over time. The way we travel on literal trips is also likely to compare with how we travel through life.

As I said before, the feeling of love is important to get a relationship off the ground, to begin a journey together. But character and love-in-action is what sustains a loving relationship. In this chapter, we'll explore several aspects of traveling in a relationship that help us determine how *lovingly* we travel together.

We'll also explore how traveling in a marriage is related to literal travel, adding to what we've already learned about updating our road map, resetting our GPS, and cleaning out our emotional baggage.

Of utmost importance when traveling with someone to some exotic destination, across town, and especially through life are

- choosing your companion,
- dealing with problems,
- being sensitive to each other's needs, inclinations, and preferences,
- complementing each other,
- being honest and trustworthy, and
- enjoying the journey.

Choosing Your Companion

If you've already made a marital commitment, it may seem too late to do much about choosing your traveling companion. But this is absolutely untrue. Although you chose to travel with this person some time ago, you must keep choosing them every day if you're to fully enjoy the journey.

It's not like anyone forced you to travel with your mate. You chose to take this trip—likely the biggest trip of your lifetime. Being mindful of this is a big deal. Too many people excitedly choose to and vow to travel life with someone only to grouse about their choice later.

If you've already started the journey, this is no time to complain. Take responsibility for your choices and make decisions for how your future together will look. Now is the time for a full-time, full-body, full-minded decision and to stand behind it.

How might you stand behind it? Spend your time and energy reminding yourself you made the right and best choice when you chose your mate. It's imperative that you choose your mate again and again no matter how difficult your relationship is in the moment. It's not enough to say "I do" at the start of a relationship. You must say "I do" again and again, each step of the way. You say "I do" to owning your part in the struggles. You say "I do" to embracing your mate for who they are. You say "I do" for doing your part to make the relationship better. Choose again to say and mean "I do."

Carrie

Carrie came to see me filled with resentment. While she'd chosen to marry Karl only five years earlier, she was miserable. Her mind and heart were flooded with questions about why she married him and how she might now leave him.

"I don't like my husband," she stated. "I wish I did, but I don't. There are so many things about Karl I don't like, and I don't know if I can get past them. I don't know what to do."

"Tell me more," I said.

"Well," she said haltingly, "I feel trapped. We have two young children, and I gave up my career to stay home and care for them. I don't feel like I have any choice but to stay with him."

"Why do you want to leave him?"

"He's mean. He snaps at me when he's upset. He's impatient and irritable much of the time."

"So how are you working on things with him?"

"I don't know if I want to work on things with him," she said, obviously irritated. "I told you. I don't like him."

"I know, but you have to decide if you're going to work on your marriage. It's a decision you have to make."

"If I choose to do that, Karl has to do his part. I doubt he will, but isn't he also responsible for where our marriage is?"

"Of course. I would hope he might join you in this work. But our first task will be helping you work on the marriage in ways *you* can."

"Seems like I can't work on him, then."

"Partly true and partly not. You can't change him, but you can work on how you approach him, how you share expectations, and how you set boundaries. You can do a lot to work on this problem without him."

"I didn't really expect you to say that."

I smiled and added, "You must begin by deciding to choose him again. You can decide you want to improve your marriage rather than just coping with the way it is now."

"Okay," she said slowly. "I guess I can do that."

Carrie looked at me like she expected me to wave a magic wand and make her like her husband.

"Do you still enjoy aspects about Karl?" I asked. "I suspect you used to like many things about him. Maybe you could work on embracing those qualities again."

"Maybe," she said. "I feel so resentful toward him. But you're right. He's not all bad."

"Let's start there. Then we might take a look at setting healthy boundaries, sharing needs and desires with him, and finding a way to invite him into this counseling process. People come to me all the time not liking their mate. Some come after their frustrations have turned into attitudes. Some come after attitudes have worked their way into bitterness. Some decide to work on eliminating the irritants they can and explore the roots of their resentment. Sometimes they find their mate isn't at the root of the problem at all."

"I know that seems unlikely now," I added, "but I hope you'll be open to exploring your attitudes."

Carrie ultimately decided to explore her feelings toward her husband. It was hard work, but she displayed flexibility and insight. She studied her mixed feelings, which are common to most people, and discovered she'd been rehearsing her resentment. She'd lost sight of the fact that she'd chosen to be in this relationship and that she could continue to choose it—or not.

Treat Your Mate with Understanding

Thank God the way we view our mate isn't etched in stone any more than how we view anyone is. We have the capacity of altering our point of view, our attitude, and subsequently the way we treat others. Of course, the way we treat others will impact how they treat us.

The apostle Peter has interesting counsel for us. Although he was addressing men, this Scripture applies to everyone: "Treat your [mate] with understanding as you live together" (1 Peter 3:7 NLT). What does this mean? How can we cultivate understanding as we travel together in marriage?

I believe Christie does a superb job of this, especially when it comes to travel. Several times I've heard her tell friends something along these lines: "David gets anxious when we travel, and it doesn't bother me to get to the airport ahead of time for his sake. It's not my preference, but I understand his anxiety, and it's easy for me to adjust my preference for him."

Consider Christie's actions. She could just as easily push for her preference, scold me for being so anxiety-ridden, and argue about the "rightness" of getting to the airport later rather than sooner. Instead, she shows tolerance and understanding.

Another way to illustrate understanding is to show your mate acceptance. This is simple advice with far-reaching implications, especially when you're experiencing tension between you. Step back and consider who you married. Consider their unique qualities and why you initially chose to be with them. Appreciate who they are and the qualities you still admire. Reminding yourself of those qualities may be enough to begin to shift your attitude toward them.

You didn't marry your clone, and you wouldn't really want someone exactly like you, would you? While it may sound tempting, I assure you you'd be bored out of your mind in no time.

Again, think back to the qualities that initially attracted you to your traveling companion, including any still alive and well in them now. Then consider why you might choose them again. Savor the feelings that exercise brings you, then, yes, choose them again!

Change Your Mind

I told Carrie she could change her mind, which means changing direction. This is a powerful insight. We all have the ability to change our attitude, and in doing so we can feel much better about our circumstances. The landscape during our travel changes. We can feel empowered to impact our lives for the better.

Have you ever heard of neuroplasticity? It's the ability of the brain to adapt and change. You may be wondering what that has to do with you, and the answer is a lot.

If you're anything like Carrie, wondering how you ended up with someone you're not sure you like, be encouraged. You *can* like them again. You can change your mind, your outlook, and your attitude, which can have a powerful impact on your relationships.

Carrie can probably learn to like her husband—or at the least limit the resentment she feels toward him. She can also impact his attitude and behavior toward her by interacting with him in strategically different ways.

In his book *Hardwiring Happiness*, Dr. Richard Hanson explains how this works:

> The brain takes its shape from what the mind rests upon. If you keep resting your mind on self-criticism, worries, grumbling about others, hurts, and stress, then your brain will be shaped into greater reactivity, vulnerability to anxiety and depressed mood, a narrow focus on threats and losses, and inclinations toward anger, sadness, and guilt. On the other hand, if you keep resting your mind on good events and conditions...pleasant feelings, the things you do get done, physical pleasures, and your good intentions and qualities, then over time your brain will take a different shape, one with strength and resilience hardwired into it, as well as a realistically optimistic outlook, a positive mood, and a sense of worth.[4]

Whew! That's a lot to take in. But what Dr. Hanson describes is being replicated by many contemporary researchers. We're capable of changing our brain and our mind.

Is this a magic wand for eliminating all problems in a relationship? Of course not. But balancing out negative thoughts and troubling emotions with more positive possibilities can only help our situation.

So when it comes to your traveling companion, it's important to choose your mate, again and again. Realizing that you have the power to impact how you interact with them can change everything.

Dealing with Problems

Another critical aspect of choice, especially as it pertains to being a good traveling companion and mate, has to do with how you deal with problems that arise during travel.

Recall that Christie and I traveled down the same road in Mexico not once, not twice, but three times before we finally changed course. Developing somewhat of a sour attitude, I suggested we abort our weekend trip after reaching the same dead end for the third time. But Christie suggested we continue, on a new route.

I also shared about our trip to where we call "the Greece you don't see in pictures." Between us, Christie had the better attitude. She suggested we make the best of our situation.

I didn't readily approve of her ideas in either situation as I was working up to a foul mood. Thankfully, Christie was the better traveling companion. She was wise enough to see that the situations were what they were and there was no sense in making matters worse by being in a bad mood. She wisely reframed our circumstances, changing our travels from colossal failures to exciting adventures. She helped me shift from feeling discouraged to openly embracing the unknown. This made a huge difference.

We have an informal motto at The Marriage Recovery Center, which we advise every couple to embrace: *We're in this together, and we can figure this out!* This is a powerful statement. Let's tease it apart:

- *We're in this together.* Whatever situation you find yourself in, you're in it with your mate. Problems become opportunities to work together as partners.

- *We can figure this out.* While no perfect solution to your problem may exist, every problem can be overcome. You can lock arms and figure out what to do about any issue, no matter how complex, and in doing so you can gain a feeling of togetherness.

The motto suggests we are a team, and in marriage, we share in either the victory or defeat. We win together or we lose together, but *we are together*. When it comes to working on a relationship, we celebrate every step of progress and gently address any points of regression.

Two people choosing to travel together must agree at the onset of their trip that problems will be *faced together*. Missed flights, delayed trains, missed meals, or the occasional stay in a super low-budget motel are inevitable. It happens. But with a bit of resilience, a troubling situation can become a laughable memory in the years ahead.

Yet What's the Problem—Really?

But if we're in this together and we can figure it out, then getting hung up must mean something else is going on.

Consider this: If two people agree to work together on whatever situation arises yet the problem persists, there may be a problem beneath the problem.

My friend Lee is one of the most mild-mannered people I know. But when I go to him with a problem, he gets right to the point and nearly always says, "Step back. The problem you're describing is not your real problem. You're telling yourself a *story* about the problem."

Look again. Have you faced your problem squarely, objectively? Is it the real problem? Or are you just telling yourself a story? And if you are, do you know what the real problem is so you can address it?

Now consider this: Lee also says—and I agree—that anything can become terrible when we tell ourselves it's terrible.

Regarding our dead-end experience in Mexico, when I told myself we'd wasted a lot of gas and much valuable time, I was miserable. But when I told myself we'd had an exciting adventure and seen some beautiful sights, the situation wasn't so bad.

Christie and I have told others about our journey aboard the Greek freighter with much delight when we could have portrayed it as a disaster. But we're both fond of sharing about the horrific meal we had, the bunk beds deep in the belly of the ship, and not seeing the Greece depicted on postcards and travel websites. We're entertained by those memories, and so are our listeners.

This illustrates that in any challenging situation, we have an opportunity to change our mind-set, allowing us to problem-solve from a different part of our brain.

Being Sensitive to Each Other's Needs, Inclinations, and Preferences

The next strategy for traveling well together is being sensitive to the other's needs, inclinations, and preferences. In short, leaving no room for outright selfishness.

Traveling with a partner is a series of compromises, adjustments, and concessions. When each of two people push for their own way, a fight is sure to ensue. Rather, using emotional sensitivity, one learns that saying "I do" sometimes means learning to go with the flow.

Christie and I recently spent a weekend at a nearby beach town, a romantic getaway to celebrate my birthday. We carefully chose our destination based on a fabulous trip a couple of years ago.

As soon as we arrived, we noticed the main street was under construction, many of the shops we looked forward to visiting were gone, and some restaurants were closed. The town no longer had the magic we remembered.

"Eek. Do we have to stay? Can we go somewhere else?" Christie asked.

"But we came to see *this* town," I said, protesting the idea of giving up—even though I felt disappointed myself. After all, it was my birthday.

"But there's really nothing to see here."

Sensing her disappointment and suppressing my desire to push for staying, I paused and gave myself a bit of emotional space to think. This attitude was a bit unlike Christie, and I was confused by it. Still, I could push and probably get my way, or I could give in to her preference. The correct answer is obvious, right?

I suggested exploring a nearby town where we knew there would be a flea market, a garden shop, a café, and the biggest cinnamon rolls on the West Coast. The combination turned out to be a big hit. Success is often the case when we're flexible and sensitive to each other's needs and preferences.

Bad Moods in Small Spaces

What do you do when an emotional hiccup occurs while traveling on a trip? Well, I was moody on the third excursion down the road in Mexico that led to a dead end, and I was cranky at being escorted into the depths of a freighter when a delightful cruise ship had been advertised for our trip to Greece.

It's unreasonable to always expect smooth travels. My guess is that's why someone invented shock absorbers—for the bumps in the road. What are you to do when life presents you with dead ends and U-turns? What are you to do in marriage, like when your mate forgets some important event—again?

While I handled the beach town getaway like a champ, I don't always do as well. I have a propensity to pout when things don't go the way I hoped—a trait I'm working on, diligently.

Imagine a different outcome. Imagine I had been inflexible. Imagine Christie being equally inflexible. Imagine a power struggle followed by my bad mood. Sounds like a horrible combination, right?

Yet this is exactly how many people travel through marriage, constantly recovering from the last painful encounter and bracing for the next. A bad mood in small spaces, where we rehearse being wronged and vilify our mate in our mind, leads to disaster. Rehearsing our self-righteousness offsets little when it comes to emotional pain. Hurting our mate with our mood is hurting our mate.

You know what I'm talking about. You, too, have experienced the effects of the bad mood someone in your family developed—your mate or perhaps your child. A bad mood brings down the collective mood of everyone around the person in the bad mood. Try as you might to avoid allowing their bad mood to impact you, it's a lost cause. We ultimately travel together, and so the mood of one impacts the mood of all.

When traveling together on a literal journey, then, or simply nav-igating life with others, take stock of the impact your mood has on those around you—especially your mate. You're not hiding your bad mood as much as you might think. Take responsibility for the fact that your mood has the power to either lift up those around you or bring them down.

The Perfect Travel Companion

If being moody, selfish, and insensitive are sure ways of spoiling an outing, how should we travel together?

In his article "9 Traits of the Perfect Travel Companion," writer Anders Carlson starts right off by saying, "The right travel partner can make or break a trip."[5] (Sounds like Mr. Twain!)

I suggest we adapt four of the ways Carlson thinks we can be ideal travel companions to describe the perfect marriage companion. See what you think.

A perfect marriage companion:

1. *Stays positive.* Finding some pleasure in most everything encountered, no matter how small or unsettling, makes a big difference when it comes to preserving a good mood.

2. *Goes with the flow.* Like missed flights or faulty reservations, changed plans or occasional missteps don't cause alarm or pouting.

3. *Encourages new experiences.* Saying yes to new opportunities creates memories, and a mate who encourages taking them can keep your trip exciting.

4. *Is willing to go his or her own way at times.* It's okay to do things or explore separately sometimes and in some ways. Each marriage partner should appreciate that opportunity. Then you can come back together to share those experiences.

You can see how each of these qualities helps get you to the place of being sensitive to the inclinations, pleasures, and preferences of your travel companion. Bear in mind you could always go it alone and do your own thing, but that's no fun.

Complementing Each Other

Perhaps you've heard the phrase "Your partner should complement you, not complete you." Said another way, you may believe your mate must think the way you do, share the same beliefs you do, and enjoy the same things you enjoy.

Not true.

At some level, we're all looking for someone who won't simply agree with us but will improve and expand us in some way. For that to occur, they must be different from us. They must be willing to challenge us to do things differently, and we must be open to that challenge.

My wife recently suggested we have her whole family over for a celebratory summer outing. While that sounded like a wonderful idea at first, I started doing the math. She has seven brothers, all with wives and children. I do value family, connection, and celebration, and I do like her family. But I suddenly felt overwhelmed.

Then I paused to reflect on her idea. Christie's inclination to celebrate with the whole clan complements my tendency to limit us to smaller, more intimate gatherings. Our family get-togethers—some bigger and some smaller—are perfect examples of complementing each other and encouraging each other to stretch in some way.

How do you complement your mate and how do they complement you? Remind yourself that finding someone just like you would be like looking at your mate every day only to see what's already in your mirror. *Boring.*

So the next time you grouse about your mate being different, consider that you chose them *because* they're different. You wanted to team up with someone who would challenge you, to help you be better on a team than alone.

We want a mate who will help us learn, heal, and grow.

Being Honest and Trustworthy

You know the type—someone who's always agreeable even though you know they really want something else just below the surface. You're left to guess what they want to do, where they want to go, and how they want to travel.

My mother was like that, and it irked me.

"What do you want to do today, Mom?" I would ask her.

"Whatever everyone else wants to do."

"That's nice, but what do *you* want to do?"

"Oh, I'm just along for the ride," she'd persist, refusing to assert her preference. I would give my wife a knowing, irritated glance.

My mother made the mistake of thinking that "going along with everyone" is a virtue, but that's not the case. We want and need to know what others think, what they prefer, and what has meaning for them—especially our mate. We want them to be *honest* with us.

Another aspect of honesty—besides, of course, not telling lies—involves being honest with yourself. We often believe we prefer one thing when the opposite may be true. Take this recent conversation with my friend Lee.

"I want to learn to tango," I told him over a cup of coffee.

"No you don't," he said, swirling his latte.

Looking at him with more than a bit of annoyance, I said, "Well, yes I do. I actually *do* want to learn to dance the tango."

"No, you really don't." Now he was grinning.

I grew more annoyed at his audacity in saying such a thing to me. His smile suggested that perhaps he was messing with me in some way. But he wasn't.

"I don't know why you're saying this, Lee. How do you know what I do or don't want to do?"

"Easy. If you really wanted to learn the tango, you'd be taking lessons. Since you aren't, you don't."

It took a few moments for his thoughts to sink in. Could he be right? Or was he misguided?

"Hmm, I'll have to think about this," I said.

I let the topic drop, but then I spent the next several days thinking about his words. Could they be true? I decided he was right. I accomplish what's important to me and procrastinate on what's not so important to me. I share my intentions with people, but they have the ring of disingenuousness to them, leaving people to wonder what I truly think and believe.

Lee's words rang in the back of my mind for days, and then they became more pronounced when I met with a friend who was taking tango lessons with his girlfriend.

"Tell me about your dance lessons, Gregg," I said, sipping iced tea on his deck overlooking Seattle. I was determined to explore the concept of honesty and choice.

"It's really fun," he said, "but it's also a lot harder than I thought it would be. And it's a huge commitment. Still, I've committed to taking lessons every Thursday evening. The instructor is great, though. Patient."

"How many lessons have you had?"

"We've been taking lessons for months, so I guess we've taken a dozen lessons or so."

"And you've improved?"

"Absolutely. And my girlfriend and I have grown closer." He paused. "But not without a few hiccups in the process," he said, laughing. "I've been tempted to quit several times, but it's important to me. I'm going to stick with it."

Hmm. Truth be told, I'm not ready to commit to taking dance lessons, and learning this kind of honesty serves both me and Christie. It's important. I'm able to speak more clearly and convincingly to her and others about what I really want to do and what I'm equally committed to doing—or not doing.

I'm impressed by Gregg. Who wouldn't be? Here's a fifty-year-old man who can hardly put two feet in motion without stumbling, taking instruction from a younger teacher. He's an established professional, having spent thirty years honing his trade, now becoming a student again.

What I admire most about Gregg, though, is his attitude. He's not grousing—well, mostly not grousing. He's open, willing, and humble as he's learning something new.

I can hear the wheels grinding in his brain, because the brain likes old patterns. If his brain could talk it would say, "What are you doing? You know how to be the professional you've trained to be. Why are you making me learn something entirely different?" The brain likes repetition, patterns, and similarity, and here he was throwing a curveball at it.

Admitting that you need to be a learner to have the love life of your dreams is a critical step. It means being open to new paths, new information. It means being open to adventure and journeying toward the occasional dead end.

This brings me to the importance of being trustworthy.

I'm reminded of the story of Moses, once a handsome and powerful prince of Egypt, then an old, forgotten shepherd. But God had bigger things in store for him. Though Moses was filled with insecurities, God chose him to lead the Israelites on a new path, out of bondage and into freedom and the promised land.

You might think the people would all jump at the prospect of being free, but that wasn't the case. And on their way to freedom, their faith was repeatedly tested. In fact, they often complained, wishing to return to bondage in Egypt rather than suffer some of the hardships they experienced on the trip. Their old familiar path appeared more comfortable than this wild journey into the unknown.

How soon they forgot the miracle they'd experienced. The Israelites had been pursued by Egyptian soldiers as they fled Egypt. Imagine their fear as they were pushed into the Red Sea with Pharaoh's armies pressing in! But Moses trusted God, and the sea was parted, leading them ever closer to freedom. Pharaoh's armies were then swallowed by the raging waters.

While trust is perhaps not so dramatic for us—and, of course, no one is God—the issue is the same: Will we let go of what we've known and trust a new way, a new route? And will we be a trustworthy mate as we journey through marriage?

Enjoying the Journey

Our final counsel on becoming a good traveling companion in marriage is to enjoy the journey. This is perhaps the most important aspect of being the best companion you can be.

While enjoying the journey is certainly cliché, it is also critically important. After all, if we're not enjoying the journey, what's the point? Furthermore, what kind of companion are we? We must find a way to adjust our attitude, so we're pleasant to be around no matter what's going on.

The problem is not the bumps in the road but how we handle those bumps. Bumps come along for everyone, no matter what partner we've chosen. Though the strategies in this chapter are sure to help, there is no perfect traveling companion. Rather than holding on to the belief that the journey would be smoother with someone else, somewhere else, we need to look in the mirror. Have we really embraced the journey as opposed to only eyeing the destination?

Enjoying the marriage journey means seeing each day as a gift, an adventure unfolding before you. Noticing exactly where you are and appreciating the blessing of being there. Facing all life's challenges with the person you've chosen. Taking responsibility for your life, recognizing that you've crafted it to look the way it is, and you can change it for the better.

And So, What About Love?

As we continue our journey toward a love life of your dreams, we realize the feeling of love is certainly important, setting the stage for all that follows in a marriage. But being a good traveling companion is critical to maintaining that feeling of love. You can love your mate intensely, but if you're a poor traveling companion, selfish and moody, you're in for a rocky journey.

So travel well. Enjoy the scenery and embrace dead ends that challenge you to make U-turns. Lock arms with the one with whom you've chosen to travel. Smile at the emotional speed bumps, and always be a learner.

Let's move forward again, this time to explore the importance of catching "the shift" that signals trouble is near.

4

SHIFTING AND MAKING YOU-TURNS

Navigating Your Journey

*If travel is like love, it is, in the end, mostly because
it's a heightened state of awareness, in which we
are mindful, receptive, undimmed by familiarity
and ready to be transformed. That is why the best
trips, like the best love affairs, never really end.*

PICO IYER

As I recall, we were on the third trip down Dead-End Lane when I could no longer contain myself. Rather, I could no longer contain my Self. I wanted to turn around and go home. In a mood, a growing funk, I lost perspective. I had shifted gears, and not in a good way.

This shift—when we lose perspective, when we're no longer able or perhaps even willing to stay fully present—is what this chapter is about. We'll explore the need to make what I call a "you-turn" when we hit a dead end, and we'll explore what I call "the shift."

The shift—from calm to concern to crisis, all in seemingly one motion—is an experience we all know. We feel our bodies change, preparing for something horrible to happen even if what we're facing is quite benign. Our heartrate quickens, our pupils dilate, and our breathing becomes shallow.

The shift—when we're no longer fully present and our energy is focused on self-protection—means we're no longer grounded and giving our full attention to our mate. We're expecting something awful, yet we pull apart from the one we care about and who can possibly offer us comfort at this time in our journey.

The journey I'm talking about, of course, is marriage, the place where presence is necessary for intimacy. But sometimes little seems to go as planned, and this shifting, this pulling apart, has significant repercussions. This deeply personal space is where we're challenged to dig deep within ourselves so the initial rush of joy we felt at the beginning of our relationship can be rekindled.

Remember, it's easy to be connected during the initial flurry of love, but it's more difficult when our emotions fluctuate as issues arise. That rush of love at the start drew us to our mate, but it isn't enough to keep us attached to this person we married. We must do more and be more.

Preparing for Shifts

On that dead-end road with Christie in Mexico, I forgot everything I knew about the responsibility of being an enjoyable traveling companion. I forgot about asking for help when I needed it. I forgot the importance and delight of being fun and lighthearted. I had shifted, my frontal cortex gone silent, giving way to my brainstem, which wanted to scream, "Take me home!"

And I most certainly was not in a mind space to appreciate Pico Iyer's notion of traveling with a sense of being "mindful, receptive, undimmed by familiarity and ready to be transformed." I was quite the opposite: mindless, closed to possibilities, certainly dimmed by familiarity, and completely unreceptive to being transformed. All that I espouse and embrace was lost, and an entire weekend hung in the balance.

Thankfully, Christie saved the day. She was ready to be transformed, and she nudged me into a healthier place. After I changed my mind and my mood, we were able to enjoy our adventure.

Someone wisely said, "If you want safety and predictability, stay home." And since this applies to marriage as well, let's stop to think about this.

Who of us, upon hearing those words before starting our marriage journey, would have contemplated "staying home" instead? Not many of us. Deciding to wed, we confidently announce that we understand problems will come, but, hey, we're ready for them. Yet then when even minor infractions occur along the way, we cry, "Unfair!" And we scream if infidelity, financial instability, emotional abuse, or deception arise. We rail when faced with a mate addicted to alcohol, drugs, or internet shopping, as well as when faced with betrayal or rejection.

Why is calm in the face of a bump in the road or an unexpected dead end so challenging? One reason is we're not prepared for encountering them. On our weekend trip, I had forgotten what I knew. I had failed to prepare.

Effective Preparation

Understanding we can never fully prepare for the adventure called marriage—and that's part of the excitement—we *can* prepare for bumps in the road and unexpected dead ends, whether their challenge is minimal or extreme. Here are some thoughts on what effective preparation for your marriage journey requires:

1. *Making a commitment.* If you leave yourself an out at the start of your marriage, chances are good you'll take it when the going gets tough—or at least be inclined to do so. Instead, make the commitment. (And if you're already on this journey, stay committed.)

2. *Shifting from "me" to "we."* Tiring of traveling solo and committed to coupleship, you must move from thinking in terms of "me" to "we." This shift must and will influence everything you think and do in your marriage.

3. *Learning and practicing effective communication skills.* Part of journeying together is communication. You can't completely withdraw communication from your mate for any length of time, in any way, without impacting the integrity of the relationship, and the communication must be effective.

4. *Deciding to make decisions together.* You and your spouse will face myriad decisions about your life together, such as with money, children, sex, jobs, and home life. Decide from the start to make those decisions together rather than striking out on your own or simply demanding your way without discussion.

5. *Cultivating companionship.* In part, we begin the marriage journey because we don't want to travel through life alone. And the sights and sounds of traveling are multiplied when we're traveling with a special person. Now that you have someone with whom you can share both the joys and challenges of life, work on developing true companionship. It will help you address—or even avoid—bumps in the road and unexpected dead ends.

Preparation is critical for our most important journey, and excellent planning at the front end can eliminate untold problems down the road.

Qualities and Skills for Preparation

In their article "The Best Preparation for Marriage: Qualities, Skills, and Right Questions," Linda and Charlie Bloom write, "Great relationships aren't discovered; they are created. Anyone with sufficient motivation and a willingness to do the work that is required for a successful relationship is capable of achieving this regardless of their background, personal history, personality, or predispositions."[6]

As indicated in the title of their article, the Blooms go on to state preparation for marriage comprises three major parts: developing essential qualities, cultivating the necessary skills, and asking the right questions.

While Christie saved the day and our weekend trip, other experiences we've had were ruined for lack of cultivating the right qualities, developing the right skills, and asking the right questions. This lack of preparation led to "the shift" in our marriage I alluded to earlier.

What are a few of the qualities the intrepid traveler must cultivate to avoid shifts? Let's look at a list of some of the qualities the Blooms believe it takes to be a good traveling companion in marriage, teasing each apart to see how it might relate to your relationship.

Patience: Patience and the ability to tolerate frustration when things don't go as planned are critical. Things rarely go as planned, and that's part of the hazard of going on an adventure. We must be able to go with the flow in all circumstances.

Faithfulness: We must, in all circumstances, remain faithful to the adventure and to our traveling companion. Even when our mate does less than their best, which we must accommodate, we remain faithful to them.

Honesty and Generosity: Strive to speak clearly and honestly. Be generous with your time, grace, and understanding. Understand we and our mate are alike in many ways, having good days and bad days, times of delight and times of not much delight.

Now here are some of the *skills* the Blooms say we need to avert danger:

Effective Communication: Every book on healthy marriage conveys the importance of effective communication. It's that important. Knowing how to share vulnerable feelings and how to broach difficult topics is mandatory. Learning how to ask for what you need in a gentle, loving manner will stave off many challenging experiences.

Active Listening: I can't say enough about the importance of active listening. The key is the word *active*. The active listener is engaged, tuned in, sensitive to their mate. They truly care and take an interest in the daily joys and challenges of their mate.

Needs negotiation: As married couples journey together, it's incumbent on both people to clarify what they need. We can't and dare not try to read each other's minds. So we must know our needs and communicate them clearly to our mate.

Boundaries: Sometimes in marriage, our needs conflict, our hopes differ, and our preferences collide. We must travel together amicably but also let our mates know what we will and will not tolerate. These can be hard yet necessary conversations.

Appreciation and Gratitude: After making the decision to journey together, we must continue to affirm each other. We never tire of hearing we're doing a good job.[7]

Anticipating Bumps in the Road

In addition to these qualities and skills, the best traveling companion will anticipate possible bumps in the road—even possible dead ends—and promote discussing them. What are some of the questions you need to ask and have answered by your partner, if not before marriage, then now? The Blooms—and I—suggest you consider topics such as children, money, sex, in-laws, job responsibilities within and outside the home, and the role of friendships in your marriage.

Most couples I counsel have been intellectually prepared for the notion of facing problems, but they're ill-equipped to actually manage working through them so they can safely and happily continue their journey.

I recently listened to a man share about his open-road adventure on a motorcycle, and I couldn't help but notice the parallels to married life.

"Traveling on a motorcycle can't be compared to riding in a car," he said, smiling. "You're one with your machine. You feel the temperature change, riding into the foothills and mountainous areas. You smell the fresh cutting of a hay field and hear the silence as you travel through desert land. You feel the bumps in the road and must slow for dangerous curves. You listen carefully to your machine and know when something begins to go wrong. Most mistakes can be avoided if you pay attention."

"What do you do to prepare for mechanical difficulties?" I asked.

"You prepare your machine for them. With proper maintenance, you're not likely to have trouble, but like I said, if there's going to be trouble, you sense it immediately."

"And if you do?"

"You have a buddy riding with you who can help. We also know the road we're going to be traveling on. Preparation and alertness are key."

Marriage is like this, I thought. We must prepare by having some idea of what marriage requires of us, and then we must immediately make adjustments when we encounter problems rather than pretending they'll just disappear.

Watch for Warning Signs

The check engine light came on in my car several weeks ago. I was tempted to ignore it, assuming it indicated nothing serious, but the light remained on. I decided to take it to my mechanic.

"It's probably nothing," he said, resetting the mechanism. "It may have simply been a loose gas cap. Those things happen. If it comes on again, bring your car back."

The light stayed off for several days, and I breathed a sigh of relief—until it came back on, this time flashing. The engine immediately began to sputter, and I gingerly drove it back to the mechanic, thinking he'd obviously missed something the first time, wondering what he should have caught.

"It's a good thing you came in when you did," he told me. "Your coil has corroded, as have your spark plug wires. Your situation could have become much worse."

"Please fix it," I said.

Several hundred dollars later, my car is again running smoothly.

Marriage also has warning lights many people choose to ignore. Recurring problems rise, then fall, tempting couples to believe the problem has disappeared this time. Most often, however, they simply haven't risen to the crisis level, demanding immediate attention.

Remember what we've said about denial, the process of lying to ourselves about the severity of a problem. Remember that denial lures us temporarily into a calm space, only to be ambushed later by an erup-tion of some sort.

The Shift—
the Greatest Sign of Trouble

Our greatest warning sign of trouble is "the shift." As I said earlier, it can begin in our bodies, perhaps even before we have a conscious awareness of what's bothering us. The shift is that moment when one or even both partners move from a place of calm attentiveness to anx-ious or angry defensiveness.

You know the shift when you discover a betrayal by your mate. You know the shift when you're instantly angry about something they do or don't do after you've talked about it a hundred times. You know the shift when you feel repeatedly unheard, as if your words are sliding off your mate's Teflon exterior. No longer able to stay present, you're immediately transported to an earlier place, perhaps involving your mate or to an earlier affront in your life.

The shift can also occur over much more minor events—when your mate questions you, snaps at you, or you're bothered about something you don't want to be bothered about. You feel frustrated that what you want and expect isn't happening. In those moments, you move from calm attentiveness and connection to angry or irritable defensiveness. You want to push away.

The shift is real for all of us, and it *must* be managed if we're to effec-tively navigate our journey with our mate. We must recognize when we're no longer present and determine where we've gone and how we got there.

Perhaps the greatest challenge is that the shift happens in a split sec-ond while life still continues all around us. Our energies are divided between what's happening within us, what's happening between us and our mate, and to a certain extent, even to what's happening within our mate. We're flooded with unwanted stimulation, and suddenly, we must attend to what's happening within us while also attending to what's happening outside of us. This is no small feat.

Kevin and Kate

Kevin and Kate came to see me for marriage counseling, with Kate scheduling their first session. They met years ago as young realtors. Now married for eighteen years, they were both forty-five years old and the parents of three children. They also owned their own real estate company, and while financially successful, they were clearly struggling in their marriage.

They sat apart from each other, appearing anxious.

"Where do we start?" Kate asked. "Do you want to hear some background?"

"Sure," I said. "Tell me what led up to coming here."

"I've been unhappy for years," Kate shared, "but I don't think Kevin realizes it. A couple of weeks ago, I told him this is it. Either he makes some big changes, or I'm moving out."

"I'm working sixty-hour weeks to keep us afloat," Kevin interjected, "and she doesn't seem to appreciate that. I'm not working this hard just for me."

"Yes you are, Kevin," she snipped. "Don't tell me anything different. This has been going on for years. Years."

"So these problems have been going on for quite a while," I said. "Did anything in particular lead to making this appointment?"

"Like I said," Kate continued, "I told Kevin he needed to make some changes, or I'm finished."

"Like what specifically?"

"I've got a long list," Kate said, looking at her husband.

"I'd like to hear it," I said.

"Let's start with how he talks to me. He acts like he's my boss at work, and then he brings it all into our home too. I hate it."

"That's crazy, Kate. I don't boss you around," Kevin said sharply.

"I'm afraid to talk to you," she told him. "Don't you see that? I'm not making this up. C'mon. I've been telling you this for years. It's nothing new."

"I can't please you," Kevin said. "And one of us has to keep the business going."

"Don't give me that," she snapped, jumping to her feet. "I work my butt off at the company, not to mention running our kids to music lessons, sports, and who knows what all. I'm doing it all while you're Mr. Top Salesman."

"That's ridiculous," he countered, staring at her. "Why don't you sit down and talk? I want to work this out."

Kate paced around my office.

"I don't think you do," she said. "You want me to be what you want me to be. A Stepford wife. Perfect at home, perfect at work, asking nothing from you. You walk in the door and start barking orders. I've had it."

"What would you like from Kevin?" I asked her.

"I've told him over and over. He's not listening. I want his time. I want to feel important to him. I want to feel loved."

Kevin winced.

"I would do anything for you and the kids," he said. "You're not being fair. You and the kids mean everything to me."

"You're not getting it. Maybe you believe what you're telling me, but your words are hollow. They don't work for me anymore."

Both Kevin and Kate were silent for a few moments.

"Look, folks," I said, "it's obvious this problem has been brewing for some time. I'd say it's time we look not only at the issues that got you here but also at the ways you're trying to resolve matters, which clearly aren't working."

"I'm willing to do that," Kevin said, "but she's got to help me figure out how to fix things."

Kate let out another sigh.

"There you go again," she said, impatient. "You don't need me to figure this out. It's time you made some decisions and showed me you mean them. You're going to lose us if you don't."

"I don't like your threat," he said, bristling.

"Not a threat, Kevin. I mean it. Take time for me. Show me I'm important. C'mon. This doesn't have to be that hard to understand."

"Folks, let's look at what's happened today. I suspect talking this way to each other is how you try to solve problems, but this pattern must change."

I paused and let my words sink in.

"It's no wonder you both feel so frustrated," I continued. "We've got work to do."

As you reflect on Kate and Kevin's dialogue, do you feel the shift in them? Do you hear how they're in a huge power struggle and how these fights, whether overt or covert, have pushed them further and further from each other? Do you notice moments of softening, making it easier for them to connect if only they will?

Kate and Kevin had and still have a lot of work to do, but they can do it. While they're not closely connected to each other now, and they've failed to discover a way to collaborate and work together, they want to rebuild their marriage. And they can do so.

The Shift Is an
Opportunity for Change

Again, "the shift" is that moment when we leave a place of open, calm, and loving connection to our mate and enter into a closed, guarded, and often angry stance. We're no longer emotionally connected to them. Feeling betrayed, vulnerable, and hurt, we opt to push away and disconnect.

This moment of disconnection is a critical moment, for it can be a short and temporary disconnection, or, if the issue isn't resolved, it can lead to a more permanent, emotional disconnection.

The shift occurs when we feel vulnerable. Instead of feeling protected and cared for, we feel frightened, and we push away.

Here are the signs that tell us we've pushed away:

> *Fighting:* One of the surest signs that we're no longer in an emotional place where we can think clearly and be connected to our mate is the act of fighting. We know we're fighting if we're argumentative, angry, accusatory, blaming, and even threatening. While we may tell ourselves we're still connected, if we scold, threaten, or attack our mate, we've shifted and are in a fighting posture.

Flighting: Another sign is the emotional and sometimes physical act of leaving. Even when we literally stay, if we've closed ourselves from gentle listening, we've begun the process of withdrawing. And if we stay in this emotional space, we're unable to connect to our mate, and no resolution can be attained.

Freezing: A final sign is what has been called "going numb." In this emotional space, we detach so much that we simply hope the situation ends soon. We're not actively and lovingly engaged; we've numbed ourselves so we can cope.

How can we use the shift as an opportunity for change? It all begins with *awareness*. We must be tuned in to our bodies enough to recognize when and why the shift has occurred. At that instant, before the situation escalates and becomes worse, we must make a decision. We can either choose to continue listening to our mate—being sensitive to what they're feeling and needing and breathe in such a way so as to calm ourselves—or we can take a time-out.

Either way, nothing good can come from any of the three postures I've outlined unless we calm ourselves.

Shifting Gears

Perhaps you're beginning to understand the importance of noticing the shift instead of being taken off guard by it. When we're alert to the signs, we can shift gears to calm ourselves, reconnecting to ourselves and to our mate, so issues can be addressed effectively.

Remember that when we shift, we move away from our mate. We abort efforts to understand, empathize, and be loving. We move from friend and loving companion to enemy, someone to avoid or guard against. Loving connection and intimacy cannot occur while erecting defenses to protect ourselves.

So we must pay attention and always be on the alert for the shift, not only in ourselves but also in our mate. While we're not responsible for a shift in them, noticing it can be beneficial. You may be able to help your mate maintain calm, depending on the situation.

Let's remind ourselves again that one of the most important ways to enjoy this journey of marriage is to remain fully present to what's going on at any particular moment. Therefore, we must all become experts at not only noticing any shift happening within us but also noticing any shift happening in our mate. These shifts are the warnings signaling something important we must attend to is happening.

Attending to whatever is most important often requires slowing down. For instance, we may choose to stop a conversation about the problem temporarily, taking a time-out from the pressing issue. Think about it. We can't effectively tend to everything happening as fast as it's happening. With emotions whirling, both inside and outside of us, there's usually too much information to process all at once.

Imagine two people, both triggered and defensive, attempting to discuss something critically important. I usually call this a fight. Both people want to be heard. Both want to speak. Both want to impress their point on the other. Both want soothing understanding from the other. The intensity rises, adrenaline crashes into their bodies, sound thinking diminishes, and emotions escalate. Can you see the problem?

What else might calling a time-out look like? Let's look at the scene from both Kevin's and Kate's perspective.

First, they could both anticipate times when they're likely to react ineffectively. Most of us have some idea where we have a raw spot in a relationship, so we should try to be more sensitive when talking about it. Having a history of conflict, Kevin and Kate could also prepare their bodies and minds for a challenging conversation where they'll specifically express what they want changed.

Did you feel the emotion shift when Kate announced she was moving out if Kevin didn't make big changes? Did you sense Kevin reacting? Did you sense Kate reacting when Kevin said he was working for the family and not himself? Both made accusation after accusation, with neither really listening to the other. They were having a fight right there in their counseling session.

If this couple is going to move forward in their marriage, they both must watch their words carefully, recognizing and curbing provocative language likely to put the other on edge. They must use language that cultivates compassion and connection. Both are responsible for this process, and it's critical for them to steer clear of generalizations and making character attacks.

Kevin and Kate could have done a much better job at recognizing when they shifted, noting how they stopped listening and began attempting to coerce the other into seeing their point of view. Recognizing this, one or both could have suggested they take a momentary or not-so-momentary break so they could shift gears back into full awareness and presence.

This shift in action, called a time-out, is a chance for both parties to collect themselves. Both are responsible for recognizing it as a time to breathe, pray, take a walk, journal—whatever will help them somehow regain perspective.

They each must also remember the task at hand—*to stay connected and lovingly solve a problem together.* A time-out is *not* a time for them to

- gather more information to use against the other.

- rehearse how wronged they've been.

- look for a way to "win," as tempting as that might be when they feel agitated. If one "wins," both lose. Once the connection between a couple is broken, it takes even more energy and grace to restore trust. And mindfulness is critical. With mindfulness, they can be alert as to whether they're connected or just trying to "win" the other over.

This *is* a time for them to

- remind themselves that their number-one goal is to journey well together, and the only way to do that is for each of them to be a good team player. If one succeeds at dominating or intimidating the other, resentment is sure to brew beneath the surface.

- reflect on what caused or triggered the shift. What did the other say that was so upsetting? Why was it so upsetting? Was some event from their past triggered, still clamoring for healing?

Kevin and Kate want to save their marriage, which means saving each other. It means taking good care of themselves and each other. When they do this, they'll be ready to fully re-engage. They can know when they've shifted back to a place where they can return to the conversation fully present, lovingly and generously available.

Having mastered the art of being so aware of yourself that you know when you've shifted into fighting, flighting, or freezing, you can then choose to shift gears to settle yourself and seek a place of loving connection.

Wrong Turns/Correct Turns

How do you know you're on the correct road? If you're clear about your destination—a healthy connection to your mate—you can determine if your actions are leading toward or away from that goal. You will likely *feel* connected or disconnected from the person you married.

Yes, much of this comes down to a feeling. A sense about things. You know the right way when you feel calm, peaceful, and loving with your spouse. You'll feel an energetic, kind compassion toward them. When you think of them, you smile. You believe all is right with the world. You're content. This is a correct turn.

When you feel edgy, irritable, frustrated—a shift—conversations in this state nearly always lead to a dead end. They take us nowhere. While we may pride ourselves in thinking we know where we're going, when honest with ourselves, we must admit this isn't true. We are, in fact, moving further away from our mate. And tension, dissatisfaction, and irritation often lead us away from not just our mate but also from ourselves.

Fortunately, we can often know immediately if we've taken a wrong turn. How can we know? Remember, you can become more sensitized to feeling connected or disconnected from your mate. If you choose *not* to make repairs to your relationship or reconnect after having said or done something hurtful and sensing "the shift" in your mate, you're turning away from your mate. One wrong turn made after another leads to dead ends, distance, disengagement. Before long you're hopelessly lost and painfully alone.

The answer to this disconnection is to take care of yourself so you can take care of your mate and your marriage. You have opportunities to make good choices, to make correct turns back toward your mate.

Once the shift has occurred for us, what are some ways to personally navigate it and find our way back? We've already mentioned some of these tactics, but they bear repeating in this context.

Slowing down: Since we feel much faster than we think, it always makes sense to slow down the process. Asking for a few moments to think during a shift is a good choice so you're not overwhelmed by emotion.

Calming down: Taking time to allow our central nervous system to relax is a great way to tame the shift. Allowing a bit of space between us and our immediate situation allows us the opportunity to think more clearly and make better choices.

Praying: We have another great resource to handle any shift—prayer. Stepping outside ourselves, we ask God to come into our situation and intervene, and He promises to guide us. The apostle Paul reminds us of the power of sincere prayer: "The prayer of a righteous person is powerful and effective" (James 5:16).

Doubting ourselves: As was the case with Hannah, the twice-married woman who knew her approach to love wasn't working, there's a time and place to doubt ourselves. Sometimes when we feel headstrong and willful, we don't know how to step out of our own way. Filled with anger and self-righteousness, we often persist in a particular direction, becoming even more lost. Doubting ourselves creates a little inner space to listen to and hear wise counsel.

Asking for direction: Left to our own wisdom, we often make decisions based on fear or hurt. Too often we're not thinking clearly, and we need others to help us regain perspective. Seeking counsel from someone uninvolved is a great way to collect our thoughts. We must find someone we trust, who seems healthy and capable to serve as a mentor offering suggestions for a better direction.

Trying a new direction: When what we've been doing isn't working, it's time to try a new direction. Too often we're reluctant to give up tried-and-true paths, remaining dedicated to the old road we've been on. But this hasn't served us well, and it's time to take some risks and try something new.

Making a You-Turn

None of us are going to do marriage perfectly. We will make mistakes. Fortunately, we often have a chance for a do-over, the opportunity to make a "you-turn" and correct our course. This is a particularly powerful tool.

Recently, I was frustrated with my wife. Actually, Christie was initially frustrated with me. She'd been out running an errand when I decided to spontaneously go to the gym for a Sunday afternoon workout. And then I just left—without even leaving a note.

Wrong move.

When I returned, she appropriately shared her disappointment with me.

"That was inconsiderate," she wisely told me. "I wish you would have told me where you were going."

Without slowing down or pausing to reflect on her words, I blurted out my selfish reaction. "I didn't know where you were. I wasn't sure what you were doing."

These were just excuses, and they propelled me further from her. Taking responsibility would have been the correct turn.

She walked away from me in frustration.

Inside I knew I was wrong, but I was caught in self-righteous justification. In a short time, I made a you-turn. I humbled myself and approached her.

"Can I try that again?" I asked.

"Yes," she said tentatively, no doubt expecting another flurry of explanations.

"I'm sorry. I didn't consider your feelings or how I would like to be treated if the situation was reversed. I thought only of myself. I was wrong, and I won't do that again."

"Thank you," she said graciously.

Defending myself is a pattern I'm trying to break.

The you-turn is a tool where we stop, admit our mistakes, consider our situation, and make corrections, and it's a tool we must use in our relationships. We make mistakes, and that's to be expected. How we handle them is most critical. If we make a pattern of defending, explaining, and justifying, we travel further away from our destination of intimate connection with our mate. Humbly admitting wrong brings us back into relationship.

What Change Requires of Us

Catching the shift, then making you-turns and heading in the right direction, is all easier said than done. These acts require self-awareness and a dedication to the truth and to growth. However, the payoff is huge: loving connection.

Being dedicated to change is necessary. Short bursts of change will yield short bursts of improvement, but then, sadly, they'll be followed by slipping back into old patterns. You don't want that for yourself or your mate.

Dedication to change, however, demands something from us. What does real change require of us? A dedication to change typically follows a pattern. You can follow these eight steps as a way to mark where you are in the change process.

1. *Denial:* In the initial stage of facing a problem, we believe we are in complete control of our lives. We're not lost; our mate is. We don't need to change anything; they do.

2. *Anger:* Our resentment grows as our mate fails to conform to our will. But the marriage isn't working, and we can't figure out why.

3. *Bargaining:* We make minor concessions, but we don't

really think we have anything to change. We're not really lost. The map must be wrong. We might also enter counseling as a concession.

4. *Chaos/Depression:* Our resentment grows as the problem isn't quickly resolved. We slip into resignation that perhaps this is the way life will always be.

5. *Openness:* Finally, we gain a glimpse of insight. We begin to make the you-turn, seeing that our attitude and map of the world may be wrong. We become open to change.

6. *Acceptance:* We now see we're responsible for how our life has been working or not working. We see the common denominator in our relationship problems is us. It's not others needing to change to conform to our will but us needing to be more forgiving, more accepting, easier to be around.

7. *Encouragement:* We begin to see life working. Our mate responds to our more positive attitude. We see the truth in the statement, "When we change, everything changes." We feel encouraged and excited about our growth. Our sense of well-being increases. Our road map is changing, and we're seeing different, more positive scenery.

8. *Staying the course:* Now we must keep the momentum going. This, in some ways, is the hardest part of the journey. Initiating change is one thing; keeping it going is another. What got us this far must be continued if we want to keep making progress.

Where are you in the change process? Have you moved through denial, blaming others, and minimizing responsibility for your relationship challenges? Are you ready to "catch the shift" to see what it can teach you about yourself?

Change begins and ends with you, and every shift is under your control.

And So, What About Love?

While the feeling of love has everything to do with connecting to our mate, it has little to do with the importance of noticing and managing the inevitable shifts that occur in relating.

It's one thing to have an initial attraction to our mate. It's something very different to maintain our motivation, staying connected to the person we married while navigating the emotional bumps that will occur. Positive regard moves us closer to our mate, but we must stay attached, and that involves managing the shift we've explored in this chapter.

Bumps in the road happen, times when we lose that positive regard. Those times, accompanied by "the shift," are critical moments. We have such a short time to decide what to do. We can blame others and slip into denial, discouragement, and even depression, or we can face the challenge, own up, and grow. I assure you growth is the better choice. I've made both decisions, and by far I prefer making the you-turn, getting back on the right course.

Are you ready to move forward? Now let's explore the power of positive codependence, dedicating ourselves as a protector of our mate's well-being.

5

TWO HANDS
ON THE WHEEL

Partnering Together on Your Journey

*Probably the biggest insight is that happiness is not just
a place, but also a process. Happiness is an ongoing
process of fresh challenges, and it takes the right
attitudes and activities to continue to be happy.*

ED DIENER

Our weekend trip to Tequila turned out fine, not so much because of wonderful behavior on my part but because we both had a hand on the wheel—meaning, we worked together, cooperatively. We didn't settle for any outcome other than both of us being happy.

The image of two people's hands on the wheel is meant to convey a sense of excitement, cooperation, and perhaps just a dose of apprehension. It's meant to convey any journey taken together, involving at least two people, determined to take good care of themselves but equally dedicated to taking care of each other. If both people aren't happy and satisfied with the journey, neither will be fully happy.

Two hands on the wheel—both yours and another person's? This goes against the conventional wisdom of being solely in charge of your well-being. It goes against the notion that one person should lead, the other follow. In a marriage, shouldn't one sit in the driver's seat and the other alongside? How will we truly navigate this journey together with both spouses' hands on the wheel?

Both people in a love relationship need to have a voice in where they go and how they get there. Marriage is, if nothing else, an illustration in cooperation and collaboration, a journey planned together, taken together, and experienced fully together.

As I write today, Christie and I have set out on another trip. We just landed at Cape Cod, Massachusetts, and our adventure has begun with both our hands on the wheel.

Several weeks ago Christie spontaneously announced, "It's time to get away."

"Sounds great," I said. "How about Cape Cod again?"

"Lovely. Let's plan it and go."

So far, so good. We don't always land on the same vision for a trip, but this time it was unanimous. We had been to Cape Cod several times in past years, and visiting the Cape in September sounded perfect.

We agreed to travel after Labor Day weekend when the crowds would begin to thin, the weather would still be warm, and the vibe of the Cape would still be in force.

Christie was delightful as she approached this trip. Note her sensitivity to my needs while balancing care for herself as well.

"You're going to need to write some, so what a perfect place to do that," she said. "You can write every morning while I sleep in, and then we'll go out and explore during the day. When we get back, you can write for a few more hours while I edit what you've written. Then out for a nice dinner."

Please ponder her words, because they're beautiful and capture the heart and soul of this chapter.

Notice that she begins with sensitivity to my needs—my need to write. Lovely. She moves deftly into her own need—to sleep. Then she weaves in an activity that's mutually satisfying—exploring. Meandering around the Cape. Sightseeing. Stopping at thrift stores and, of course, finding the perfect coffee shop. Then back to our wonderful bed and breakfast where I can write again.

Her proposal has a cadence that may be lost on you. Picture a happy woman who is keenly aware of her needs while being sensitive to her husband's needs as well—both their hands on the wheel.

A Gentle Touch

Two people's hands on the wheel requires exquisite sensitivity to work. But what if that sensitivity isn't there? What if a forcefulness is in its place? Imagine two people guiding a car down the road like a torpedo, capable of destroying anything in its path if it's out of control.

To further understand the gravity of this situation, imagine these two people at odds with each other, fighting. Both their hands are on the wheel, their bodies surging with adrenaline and animosity? Both have a strong voice over whether the vehicle veers to the left, to the right, or straight ahead. Imagine a power struggle ensues. Picture both grabbing wildly at the wheel, the car (their marriage) now careening out of control.

Now let's infuse this potentially destructive situation with gentleness and calm. Imagine each of two people gently having one hand on the wheel, deferring to each other in love. Imagine them lovingly cooperating, both watching to the left and right, navigating away from danger and moving kindly toward their agreed-upon destination.

In the first situation is extreme danger—clutching and grabbing, a chaotic power struggle. Both are attempting to wrest control from the other, all the while creating even greater problems. Can you imagine the screeching of brakes, the burning of tires, the crash of steel against steel?

Marriage is no less fragile than two people moving through time in the same space, each life dependent on the other for a safe outcome, both their hands on the wheel gently guiding their marriage. This is the heart and soul of this chapter.

Your marriage requires cooperation and collaboration. You may not have recognized this when signing up for marriage, but these qualities must be present for a healthy relationship. A pitting of one will against the other won't work. Passive-aggressive maneuvers to overwhelm the other won't work. These simply cannot occur.

"Two hands on the wheel" demands a gentle, kind touch, each person understanding that the safety and well-being of the other is partly in their hands and that they're in this together. A good outcome depends on them both.

Two Disparate Needs

Yet this way of moving through marriage is more easily said than done. You know the human condition. Since Day One we've all been screaming and crying for what we want. To make matters worse, we're often insensitive to what those around us want. We give a nod to their concerns, a slight gesture to indicate we've heard them, but we're mostly oblivious to what's happening within them. Vaguely aware of their needs, we're not nearly as tuned in to others as we are to our own needs. And that is how we move through life, spilling into marriage.

To be fair, wanting what we want isn't wrong. We've been created to have desires. We have preferences, and we have needs. Tuning in to ourselves is, in fact, healthy. A healthy regard for ourselves is important.

Insensitivity to others is what causes the problem. When we lack true empathy, our mate's needs and wants are absent from our field of view. Their concerns are not automatically our concerns. They know it, they sense it, and then trouble begins.

This all sets the stage for significant problems. What I want clashes with what you want. Our needs are disparate, and at times they oppose each other. You know the outcome. Conflict. Tension. Sometimes even a battle.

The apostle James offered a stark warning about this: "What causes fights and quarrels among you? Don't they come from your desires that battle within you?...You covet but you cannot get what you want, so you quarrel and fight" (James 4:1-2).

As a psychologist, I'm drawn to this Scripture because it's so descriptive. James says it the way I see it—we selfishly want things to be the way we want them to be. Then when anything gets in the way of what we want, we either aggressively go after it or pout because we didn't get it. We haven't learned the gracious art of sharing, at least not yet. The outcome is harm to us and to others.

Self-Awareness

"Two hands on the wheel," working collaboratively, is how a relationship works most effectively. The key is to be so self-aware, so other-aware, that we're not tugging or pulling but gently working with the other person.

Enter the ego. If we're not fully self-aware and sensitive to our mate, we grab and jerk the wheel. We tug and pull chaotically yet still expect the car (the marriage) to run smoothly.

We should never even think about doing this, but we do! Not only do we think about it but we're cavalier in the process. *Of course I can grab the wheel and manipulate the situation. I'm entitled to steer for the course I want. I know what's best.*

This is wild, crazy talk, right? We would never fight for control of the wheel in a moving car. This would be suicidal, a bad way to die, not to mention the recklessness of placing others in danger of outright harm.

Yet I suggest you may be doing this in your marriage now, hardly aware of it. How self-aware are you? Do you recognize when you've done something akin to recklessly grabbing the wheel? How keenly aware are you of moving through the world as a passenger with someone else in a moving vehicle (your marriage)?

The key, as you can see, is self-awareness. When I liken marriage to a moving vehicle, we get a glimpse of the absurdity of a power struggle behind the wheel.

But what is self-awareness? Self-awareness is having a clear perception of your personality. This includes having a sense of your thoughts, attitudes, motivations, and emotions. Not only are you aware of these aspects of yourself, but you have a sense about them in others as well.

I call this having a sense of "I-me-we" simultaneously. Yes, it's a lot to take in, but we must cultivate this sense in marriage. First and foremost, we must monitor ourselves, then pay attention to our mate, and—this is so important—watch the interaction between the two of us. This is self-awareness.

So, then, self-awareness for me is noticing Christie's needs, inclinations, and preferences, such as on a weekend getaway on Cape Cod. When will she awaken? When will she want breakfast? It's also me paying attention to my energy and how much writing I've accomplished. Then it's paying attention to our interaction. Does Christie want to begin exploring right away? Am I ready to explore? This is an orchestrated dance, all with both our hands on the wheel.

Self-awareness is not an on-again, off-again state; rather, it's fluid. We move in and out of awareness, and in the best of circumstances, we're able to adjust our awareness to meet the needs of the moment. Of course, being tuned in to the needs of our mate will work wonders when it comes to intimacy and emotional connection.

How would you rate your self-awareness?

- I'm hardly aware of what I'm thinking or feeling, moment by moment. Being aware sounds difficult. (Low)

- I'm somewhat aware of having thoughts and emotions; I just have little practice in talking about them. But I do journal or reflect at times, which helps me become more aware of myself. (Moderate)

- I'm very self-aware, so I not only understand my emotions but I can adjust my thinking to impact my feelings. I have cultivated this skill with practice over time. (High)

How does all this relate to two hands on the wheel? Simple. If you lack self-awareness, you're likely to struggle with your mate for control. You may even be unaware that you're struggling with them, all the while wasting energy and placing both yourself and your mate in peril. Self-awareness is critical to healthy functioning.

Self-awareness is, after all, like a thermostat we tend and regulate. If we're always aware of how we move through the world, we can adjust our actions and comments to fit any situation. This has also been called emotional intelligence—knowing the right thing to say at the right time and in the right way.

What if you have a low level of self-awareness? Perhaps you're vaguely aware you're causing problems with your actions and reactions, but you feel helpless to change. Your thoughts and emotions flood in like a raging river, and you just do your best to stay afloat. What if you feel very alone and have no control over your emotions?

Sadly, this is where most of us function. We're at the mercy of our emotions, hardly aware of having any influence on them at all. We're also at the mercy of circumstances impacting our emotions. Life is a blur of reactivity. We may be aware of our thoughts and feelings and even have feelings about our thoughts and feelings. Still, we're unable to really redirect our thoughts, feelings, and actions. We remain swept up by currents of emotion.

Being aware that you're mostly unaware is an opening for change. Being aware of a need for change is a great place to start. At this point you know you must make changes in your thoughts and in your interpretations of those thoughts. As you change how you interpret life, changing your attitudes, beliefs, and how you handle your emotions will follow.

All of this, however, must be done moment by moment. Being self-aware is not a switch you flip on and then walk away from but rather a tool you adjust in response to a particular situation. You practice it in your relationship when times are tough. Using self-awareness, you can adjust how you view a situation and change the quality of your relationship for the better.

Take a moment and practice self-awareness right now. Think about what it must be like for someone to be with you today. Would your mate describe you as a fun traveling companion? Or might they say you're moody, irritable, self-centered? If you wanted to make an adjustment, what adjustment might you make?

Other-Awareness

Being aware of yourself is just the first step toward change. You must also cultivate an awareness of others in your world. Two hands cooperatively on the wheel means noting how your mate moves through the world and participating.

This is a huge challenge for most of us. We're generally self-absorbed, more or less encompassed by our myopic thoughts and emotions. Creating space for others can be a major feat. Nonetheless, accomplishing it is critical.

To take the time to reflect on Christie's needs, I first must make space within myself. I must temporarily put aside my own goals, wishes, dreams, hopes, and aspirations, which take up a lot of room in my brain. Again, this is no small feat since I'm often wrapped up in what I consider to be important.

But I want to consider my wife, as I presume you want to consider your mate. At this moment, Christie is strolling the streets of Chatham, Massachusetts, while I write somewhere away from our bed and breakfast—a nice "two hands on the wheel" move we've made with and for each other. I imagine her moving in and out of shops, people-watching, and enjoying the sunshine. She'll join me soon, and then we'll head back to our bed and breakfast for the evening.

Being aware of Christie, however, is far more than wondering what she's doing. I must be and want to be aware of what she's thinking about. What are her concerns? What are her dreams? Who is she today and how is she different from yesterday? These will be good questions for me to ask her. These are good questions for you to ask your mate.

Balancing Act

Reflecting on Christie is, of course, a dynamic process. This consideration is a dynamic, moment-to-moment effort, and it's all about balance—the give and take in the relationship. I think about her and her needs while she also thinks about me and my needs. "Two hands on the wheel" also means I give a gentle nudge in one direction at one moment and then encourage her to nudge in another direction at another time. It's all about balance.

Perfect balance, however, does not exist. Remember, this is a dynamic process. Sometimes, even for days, it's all about me. A bit of selfishness, at the right time, can be accommodated nicely. And sometimes, even for days, it's all about her. The key is balance in the relationship.

Kelly

Kelly was a sad, thirty-eight-year-old woman. She called me, stating she and her husband, Jed, were having serious marital issues and needed urgent help.

An accomplished chiropractor, Kelly had been self-absorbed for years as she made her way through college, graduate school, and building her thriving practice. Jed got lost in the shuffle. When they came to see me, Kelly had recently learned he was having an affair with someone from his work. Neither saw the affair coming, but even though they both tended to their children and their home, Kelly was working long hours, and this had become their "normal."

According to Jed, their marriage was in a state of slow death when he felt attracted to the woman at work.

"I don't know what to think," Kelly said to me tearfully during a session. "I can't stand the thought that Jed cheated on me. I would never cheat on him, no matter how lonely I was."

"I'm so sorry," Jed told her, and he appeared to mean it. "I let something happen that never should have happened."

"How could you do this?" she asked him. "We made a vow to each other."

"Anything I say will sound like an excuse, Kelly, and there are no excuses."

"But I thought we had a good marriage…"

"I didn't," Jed said. "We love each other, but we've been like two ships passing in the night. You work twelve-hour days. We coparent our kids, but that's about all we do together."

"Isn't that enough? What's more important than raising a family? My work is just my work. I thought I was building something for us."

"No," Jed said firmly. "It's not enough. Your practice has become your life. I tried to pull you away from it, but you never listened. I want a loving, healthy marriage."

"But we've always loved each other, haven't we?" Kelly asked, looking at Jed with more tears in her eyes.

"Yes, but that isn't enough."

"So it's the sex," Kelly said flatly.

"Absolutely not." Jed was clearly exasperated. "The affair wasn't about sex. It was about feeling connected to somebody."

We're all looking to be joined with someone, moving in a similar direction, caring for what they care about and feeling cared about in return. It's about feeling profoundly connected to another person. But Kelly and Jed had not been traveling with both their hands on the wheel, and now they were struggling to reconnect, to somehow weather this severe storm that was a tragic wake-up call for their marriage.

Should Jed have sounded more of an alarm? Could Kelly have listened when he complained? Yes. They should have been far more tuned in to each other. Now they've vowed to work at grieving their losses together and rebuilding their marriage. Kelly has cut back on her work schedule, and they're carving out time for some of the activities they previously enjoyed together.

Positive Codependence

In hindsight, it's easy to see where Kelly and Jed went wrong. Clearly, Kelly lost sight of Jed and their marriage in pursuit of her dream to be a health practitioner. Jed allowed feelings of resentment to linger, failing to share his needs and concerns with his wife in an effective way. Their marriage had been in trouble for some time without either calling out for help.

Their struggle is all too common. Independence has long been touted as something we should all strive for. "Be all you can be," the saying goes. It's hard to argue against that. After all, being overly dependent on our mate leads to serious problems, such as a loss of self-esteem, a lack of self-confidence, and feelings of powerlessness to ask for what we want and need in our marriage. We may have become inclined to please our mate to our own detriment.

At the other end of the spectrum is codependence, where we look to someone else to complete us. We feel insecure and vulnerable, looking to another person to make us feel whole and healthy. This never works, and it's unfair to place that burden on anyone.

Problems arise from either extreme—excessive individuality, as we witnessed with Kelly and Jed, or problems of people-pleasing. I also often see issues arising from either excessive dependence or excessive independence.

The balance we need involves neither excessive dependence nor independence but rather interdependence: two people, healthy in their own right, choosing to come together to become more than they are individually.

A term I use to describe "two hands on the wheel" is *positive codependence*, where both partners feel closely connected to the other while maintaining a strong sense of individuality. It doesn't mean being obsessed with our mate, but it does mean considering them in all aspects of our life. When positively codependent, we carry our mate with us, wherever we go. We think about their welfare in all that we do. To a certain extent it means not being okay if your mate isn't okay.

Christie is preparing to have my extended family visit our home for a day after we return from Cape Cod. It's a big deal, with twenty or so people coming to our small cottage, and we have an opportunity to really work together. She's shared some of the details of her preparation, and I've paid attention, noting the added work this suggests for her.

Being sensitive (positive codependence) means I listen carefully when she talks about the upcoming event. First, she plans her menu. I ask if there's any way I can help with that, also reassuring her the menu sounds great. And even though I suspect she'll decline when I ask if I can help with her other preparations in any way, such as with her table layout, I know she senses my interest in them, which opens up the possibility of her sharing more about her vision for the day.

Being sensitive means I listen to not only what is said but what is not said. I ask questions, gently. How is she feeling about the event? Does she feel ready? What does she need from me? How can I best support her and be an active part of the event?

Remember, "two hands on the wheel" is a moment-by-moment

thing. In some moments I must move in, offering more support. In other moments I must pull back, allowing her room to be Christie and do things the way she prefers to do them. All in all, this is about collaboration—working together toward a common goal.

Collaboration

Collaboration is one of my favorite words. Collaboration is so much more than simply cooperating with another person, as important as that is. It's recognizing that you plus someone else equals something greater than the two of you separately.

An example of collaboration exists in my business. Right now six therapists are part of my company, The Marriage Recovery Center. All six of us have differing levels of experience, training, and orientation. We're each different from the others.

But this difference is exciting. When we meet to discuss a challenging situation, new ideas always emerge. We rarely approach a situation from the same place, and we invariably arrive at differing conclusions. The results, however, are dynamic.

The same dynamic takes place in my marriage. Christie is different from me. She is, first and foremost, a woman. She also came to our marriage with a different faith tradition, a different life experience, a different education, and different preferences.

These differences, when appreciated, create excitement in our marriage. I don't think the way she thinks, and she doesn't think the way I think. When we set out to appreciate our differences and understand that we both have a hand on the wheel, the results are wonderful.

Mutuality

Add another incredibly important dynamic to the power of collaboration—*mutuality*. You don't hear this word spoken too often. In fact, I have to think about what it really means for a moment.

I know what individuality means—listening to myself and what I want and believe is best for me. And I'm learning about positive codependence—listening to the heartbeat of my mate, what she thinks about and what she wants most in her life to be satisfied.

But *mutuality* is another matter. Exploring resources to understand this concept and how it pertains to two hands on the wheel, I discovered that mutuality involves feeling secure that my mate and I are both loved equally. Mutuality means we're equal in our energy for staying together.

According to Dr. Tina Tessina, four major areas of mutuality must be present if a relationship is to succeed and grow: love, trust, benefit, and support.[8] Let's look at her definition, then break them down a bit more.

"Mutual Love: Love is the constantly renewing energy that keeps commitment alive. When both partners feel loved, and both feel appreciated for being loving, commitment can thrive."

While some of us may want to say "I love you" only once and have that sustain our mate indefinitely, those words and the meaning behind them must be renewed day in and day out.

"Mutual Trust: As promises are kept and feelings respected, trust in each other grows. In order for equality to exist, both partners must experience roughly the same degree of trust."

Trust is incredibly fragile, easily shattered, and hard to rebuild. Trust is not a once-and-for-all process, but rather, much like love, it is renewable. Take care to guard this tender quality in your relationship.

"Mutual Benefit: The benefit we gain is based on what each person knows he or she will get out of the relationship, and how each person is enhanced in the relationship... The relationship must feel similarly beneficial to both partners."

If benefit from a relationship is significantly greater to one person than to the other, trouble will ensue. Changes need to occur to achieve equal benefit for both partners.

"Mutual Support: Implicit in a loving relationship is the understanding that you and your partner will support each other—emotionally, financially, mentally, spiritually, verbally—to the best of your ability, through both good times and bad."[9]

Both partners must feel completely supported for love and

mutuality to grow. A breach in any one of these areas leads to insecurity in the relationship. Take heed to secure these areas of your relationship.

As you review this list of qualities needed for mutuality to thrive, notice the importance of having two hands on the wheel, where you determine together where you're going and how you'll get there. With both your hands on the wheel, you'll build mutual love, trust, benefit, and support into your relationship.

If you think one or more of the criteria for mutuality is missing for you, say something. Step out and share your feelings. With this list in hand, be specific with your mate about how you need the relationship to change and grow.

Sensitivity and Generosity

Mutuality can't exist without an attitude of sensitivity and generosity, so it's important to add these ingredients to a collaborative marriage.

Some time ago I happened upon a quote attributed (and often modified) to either Ian Maclaren, Philo, Plato, or Socrates: "Be kind, for everyone you meet is fighting a hard battle."

After reflecting on this quote, I vowed to walk through life mindful that everyone I met was struggling with something. This has impacted how I initially see people and how I interact with them.

While many people might appear to have it all together, this is rarely the case. Most of us are struggling with some difficulty, and we deserve and need compassion. As we listen carefully to others, we realize this is true.

Of course, in my profession, I can see that everyone has their struggles behind the façade of self-importance and titles. While this truth sometimes catches me by surprise, it always humbles me. Regardless of money, power, or prestige, everyone has their challenges, and we can have compassion for them.

A passage in Scripture tells a wonderful story that supports this notion. In it, Jesus gives a call to action for all of us.

Then the king will say to those at his right hand, "Come,

you that are blessed by my Father, inherit the kingdom prepared for you from the foundation of the world; for I was hungry and you gave me food, I was thirsty and you gave me something to drink, I was a stranger and you welcomed me…Truly I tell you, just as you did it to one of the least of these…you did it to me" (Matthew 25:34-40 NRSV).

This Scripture tells us we are to tend and care for all God's children. Everyone, when we look closely, is suffering in some way. Some physically, some relationally, but each of us in some way. Everyone is a child of God and deserving of care and compassion.

What does this have to do with marriage? I think everything. While marriage is likely the place where we feel the most challenged, and at times the most distant and guarded, sometimes the most upset and most ruffled, it's also a beautiful place to practice compassion. It's a perfect place to step outside of ourselves and offer grace to another individual.

Offering sensitivity and generosity has a powerful impact on your marriage. These are the qualities that allow you to really embrace "two hands on the wheel." When you have the power to offer more to your mate, why not do it? When inclined to withhold compassion because your feelings have been hurt, don't. Be generous and kind.

What might sensitivity and generosity look like in your marriage? Step back and consider your mate. Consider the unique challenges they're facing and how you might show mercy to them.

Believing Their Best Intentions

A corollary to serving "the least of these," which Jesus talked about in Matthew 25, is the notion of believing in the good intentions of others, especially our mate's. We can risk placing our hands on the wheel with this other person because we believe they have our best in mind. They would never intentionally harm us.

Okay, I know this might be a stretch for some of you. If you're at odds with your mate, you may have a hard time believing they care about you. But (and I ask you to stretch here) is it possible they really do care about you and want good things for you?

Studies indicate many people tend toward the negative, inclined to believe bad things are going to happen and that others want the worst for them. That's not true. While they may struggle with their own challenges, other people are *not* out to get you. In fact, they want good for you.

What might happen if you believed in the best intentions of your mate? What if you decided they really are looking out for you, are in favor of you, and hope good things for you? How might that influence how you respond to them? If you believed they had good intentions toward you, would you be more inclined to put your hands on the wheel with them?

Let's agree to move through the world believing others are fallible, like ourselves, and burdened, like ourselves, yet wish good things for us—and that this includes our mate.

And So, What About Love?

We've agreed the feeling of love is wonderful. We long for it, pine for it, and even strive for it. We even attempt to coerce or manipulate our mate into giving it to us. This, as we now know, won't work.

For love to work we must have collaboration and mutuality, sensitivity and generosity—working together to achieve everything we both want. In this orchestrated dance, this ever-renewable relationship, we remain tuned in to our mate, making adjustments as needed.

This chapter has been about both people in a marriage relationship having a hand on the wheel and the prospect of collaborating with our mate to achieve love, trust, benefit, and support. As we take great care to ensure that mutuality exists, our relationship will be enhanced, vibrant, and alive.

Let's move forward again, this time exploring what happens when we're alone in the driver's seat.

6

IN THE DRIVER'S SEAT

When You Must Travel Alone

Anything we fully do is an alone journey.
NATALIE GOLDBERG

t's always nice to have a companion when traveling. It's preferable
to share the sights and sounds of new places with someone you care
about.

But this, as you know, is not always how it goes in a marriage.

Sometimes we must travel completely alone—or at least essentially
alone. And sometimes we may not literally be alone, because we're still
married, but we *feel* alone. Our mate, for some reason (and those reasons vary) has chosen to let go of the wheel, allowing, encouraging, or
leaving us to proceed on our own. We are squarely in the driver's seat
alone.

These can be times of great confusion, upheaval, and unrest, but
they may also be times of great awakening. Times of unsettledness do
that to us—they crack us open, leaving us emotionally available to new
possibilities.

Being in the driver's seat alone can take many forms. Perhaps your
mate is preoccupied. When that happens, you're in the driver's seat

alone for only a short time. But you must still figure out how to proceed. Perhaps you're in the midst of a fight, and your mate wants space. Perhaps you're temporarily separated from your mate and must go it alone for some distance. Perhaps your mate has simply stepped back, asking you to determine a direction and check back with them later.

No matter the reason you must go it alone, you must figure out how to navigate by yourself. This what this chapter is about, and we'll explore how you can not only make the best of the situation but actually thrive.

How We Got Here

We don't attach to a traveling companion expecting to travel alone. We don't ask another person to join us for our travels anticipating pulling apart. We pair up with someone because we enjoy their company. We like the connection and make plans to travel together. When we weave that special person into our future, they become part of us, and we expect they will always be there. This is only natural.

I still remember the sudden jolt in the gut I felt a year ago when Christie asked to be alone for a time, spending several weeks in our cottage next door. I experienced confusion, sadness, and intense anxiety. What did she mean, moving next door? We were married. Connected. Sharing life together. What could she possibly mean by spending time alone?

I never anticipated her request, and like I tend to do in any crisis, I immediately wanted to reject the notion. It couldn't be true. But it was, and I soon discovered she meant business.

I didn't like it, and I didn't want to travel solo.

Still, upon reflection, it should not have been entirely surprising. She'd been unhappy with me over a number of issues. She'd voiced her displeasure, but I had taken it all in stride, hardly skipping a beat in my work and social life. Of course, this was all a huge mistake.

While Christie had been riding alongside me, she wasn't happy, and I had ignored her unhappiness. She sat in the passenger seat, but we hadn't experienced both our hands on the wheel in some time.

"I need some time alone," she said to me that day. "I need some time to think."

"What do you mean?" I asked, anxious. Her words stung.

"David," she said firmly, "I need some time to think over what I'm missing in this marriage."

This time her words hit me like a rock.

"Okay. But what does *that* mean?" I scrambled to make sense of her words, which were coming at me far too fast.

"I don't know," she said. "I'll let you know when I know, but until then, I need space."

These are the words no one wants to hear: "I need space." Many of us have heard them at some time in our lives, but they're never easy to hear. I wanted something far more definite. I wanted and sought reassurance, but it wasn't coming.

Pressing her would clearly cause more damage, which I didn't want to do. So resigned, there was little I could do but give her the space she requested.

I began my travels alone.

Traveling Alone

Traveling alone in a marriage is strangely odd and wildly uncomfortable, at least at first. It's like sitting in a car, moving down the highway, looking at the passenger seat and expecting someone to be there. You can imagine them sitting there. You can imagine what they might say, what they might do. You can, if you imagine, even *feel* their presence. This is their seat, after all. But no one is there, and the silence is deafening.

This development was terribly disconcerting, and it took a lot to get used to. This was not the way it should be. I wanted Christie there. She hadn't died, so I knew she *could* be there. But she was choosing not to be there, and this was all the more painful for me.

What could I have done to make her *choose* not to sit next to me? Was I that bad? I was initially preoccupied by doubt and shame. I played over recent weeks and months in my mind, seeking answers to overwhelming questions.

Your reasons for traveling alone may be similar or different from mine. Still, you will have to get used to the empty seat beside you. It isn't how you expected to continue your journey, but you *can* adjust. You must adjust.

Flooded with feelings of loneliness and anxiety, I coped. I wish I could say I flourished, but that wouldn't be true. Did I adjust? Yes. Did I grow more comfortable traveling alone? Yes. Did it ever feel good? No, I can't say it did.

Adjusting to being alone isn't easy. The word *adjustment* has the connotation of being a challenge. If driving alone was easy, it wouldn't require adjustment. You're living in a way you don't prefer and didn't expect, so it takes a shift in attitude to make the best of it.

Perhaps you're traveling alone emotionally, not physically. Perhaps you feel so profoundly disconnected from your mate that the idea of both your hands on the wheel feels foreign. Perhaps it's been some time since you felt the connection that comes from two people working together.

Whatever the reason, you're traveling alone. Now it's time to lean into the experience, feel it, learn about it, and make the best of it. Resisting it will only cause further suffering and delay healing. It's time to learn and grow.

Working on Your Marriage Alone

Soon enough, reality set in for me. This was really happening. I remember looking out my window and literally saying, "So this is the way it's going to be," hoping that somehow saying the words would help the reality settle in easier.

It didn't.

"This is what it feels like to be alone, to be left," I added.

The words still didn't offer any comfort. My world had drastically changed in a short time.

Perhaps your world has drastically changed as well. You might look around, like I did, and wonder if the granola will still taste the same. *Will I still want my morning latte, or will everything taste bland?* I wanted someone there to hold my hand and walk me through the adjustment being demanded of me, but I was really alone. I wanted my parents, who had died a few years earlier. I felt small and vulnerable, and my father, as tough as he could be, might have provided some kind of stability in my shaking world.

But this would be my time alone, to learn lessons I needed to learn. I needed to learn about being in a marriage alone. I needed to learn about me. This was something I'd counseled others to do, yet doing it myself was a different matter. It had become painfully personal.

I wasn't working on my marriage completely alone, of course. After all, Christie was doing *her* work, which was different from mine. Still, I felt like I was trying to repair our marriage singlehandedly.

I was also frequently overwhelmed by feelings of loneliness. You may know the feeling. Friends can be there, at times, but not *all the time*. You're faced with working on a marriage by yourself. Even if it's not literally true, you *feel* like you're working on your marriage alone.

I remember sinking into a sour attitude, bitterness just at the edge of my awareness. Why were all the problems placed on my shoulders? What happened to the notion of marriage issues being a two-way street? Didn't she contribute just as much to our problems? The more I rehearsed those sentiments, the worse I felt and the more futile everything seemed.

You may struggle to maintain a positive attitude as well, striving hard not to feel sorry for yourself. Like me, you may fight grinding away on the inequity of it all. I *did* feel sorry for myself. I struggled not to allow resentment to set in, but it wasn't easy.

I had to keep reminding myself Christie's time apart was no easier for her than it was for me. In fact, I suspect her time was equally, if not more, painful. She spent a lot of time sleeping, reflecting, and putting things in perspective. This was no vacation for her. We were both in our own pain.

In this way I was not alone. We were traveling together, down a similar road, just not in the same car.

"I want you to work on *you* while we're apart," Christie said to me.

"What?" This made no sense to me. How can anyone work on their marriage unless they're actively in relationship?

"I want you to work on you," she said again. "I'm going to spend time thinking about me, and it would mean a lot to me if you spent time thinking about you."

I still didn't understand what she meant, and it would take time for me to fully grasp what she was saying. I have subsequently learned a lot more about traveling solo and making the best of that time. In fact, lessons can be learned alone that can't be learned while connected to our mate. Many lessons can be learned only when we're alone.

I realize this may not make sense to you either, not at first. Working on a marriage seems like it should always be done with our mate. But this isn't true. I learned that the hard way, and you can learn this too.

Consider the advantages I had while working on my marriage alone:

First, *I wasn't distracted by my mate*. While I wanted to be distracted, that's not what would bring about healing. You, too, may want to be distracted, but this won't give you the time and focus you need to consider the issues you need to be considering. Being apart, in whatever sense it is for you, allows you not to be distracted. You can focus on you and the work you need to do.

Second, *I gained a new perspective*. Time apart to reflect helped me see things from other points of view. I was far more easily able to consider Christie's feelings and consider what she'd been trying to teach me.

Again, I know this may not be what you want to hear, but you too have an opportunity to gain a new perspective if you're traveling alone. Being apart, at least emotionally, allowed me to look at things from another point of view. During this time, my old routine was shaken up and tossed around, and the new had yet to be determined.

I gained new attitudes and perspectives every day I was apart from Christie. I reminded myself she still cared for me. I reminded myself this process was good for me, albeit painful. Slowly, ever so slowly, I settled into being alone and actually appreciating the time apart.

Third, *I became open to new input*. Part and parcel of gaining a new perspective is being subjected, perhaps unwillingly at first, to new information. I talked to new people, acquired new reading, thought new thoughts. In whatever way it comes to you, you have the opportunity for new input and new information—both desperately needed.

Fourth, *I accepted that what I was doing wasn't working.* It seemed like it was working, but it wasn't! My denial was strong. My life really was not working, in any sense. I couldn't go back.

If what you're doing isn't working, it can in fact be slowly killing you and your marriage. Alone, you have the opportunity to step back and see your life and marriage haven't been working, then choose not to go back and instead move forward.

Fifth, and finally, *I opened myself up to the possibility of change.* It didn't happen automatically, but it became a possibility. This crisis gave me the opportunity to explore new thoughts and attitudes.

This is your chance to try on new behaviors. You can open yourself up to change. The old is shaken up, and the new has room to come into your life. With a new mind-set and an open heart, you can work alone on your marriage. While you hadn't planned this, it can prove to open up exciting opportunities for you.

Companions During Solo Travel

Natalie Goldberg was only partly right when she said, "Anything we fully do is an alone journey." I don't know that I would ever choose an "alone journey," but this period in my life was mostly an alone journey.

Christie was on her parallel journey, and that offered me a bit of comfort; she was close by. But she wasn't close enough. I was always aware of her presence yet still separate.

Others came alongside me. If you're like me, friends, the ones you choose to call and who will be there for you, can never place a hand on the wheel of your marriage, but they can help you navigate the journey, offering much-needed comfort. I feel indebted to a few dear friends who walked me through my most challenging hours. Lee, Gregg, Tad, and Dan all did this for me. They were my go-to guys, often there by phone when the night came crashing in on me. And there were new friends too.

I found I never had to be completely alone. Many people are glad to offer a listening ear, and I offered the same for them.

Attitudes on Solo Travel

Sometimes you're driving alone and yet your mate is riding along-side—just silently. They're there physically, but they've checked out emotionally. What if your mate won't really engage with you, and they might just as well be gone?

This can be even more painful than a physical separation. The pro-verbial elephant in the room is the emotional pain that lingers like a dark cloud hanging between you. Everything you're doing has only made matters worse. Now you both suffer in silence.

This is incredibly frustrating. You know what you want to do and know where you want to go, and yet your mate refuses to participate with you. This is no time to panic, and yet that's exactly what your brain is telling you to do.

I vividly recall the panic I felt when Christie pulled apart. I knew better than to push her, but that's exactly what I did. I sent her lovely cards telling her how much I missed her. I left flowers at her doorstep, reminding her of my love for her. The only thing I didn't do—but I would have if I could—was force her back to me.

"Please, David," she pleaded with me at one point. "I need space and time. Please give that to me. You will only make matters worse if you press me."

I was giving her everything she asked for—attention, affection, gifts of appreciation—but all at the wrong time and in the wrong way. All to serve *me*, not *her*.

The last thing anyone wants is to be coerced into doing something they don't want to do. Trying to make a spouse who's pulled away return is the kiss of death. Feeling smothered, manipulated, and con-trolled, they will push away even more forcefully.

The healthiest attitude is to embrace being in the driver's seat alone. Whether or not your mate is sitting in the seat next to you, you're in the driver's seat—at least you're in *your* driver's seat.

The key is this: Control you and only you. Anytime you slip into trying to control your mate, you lose. Now is the time to focus stead-fastly on you and the work you need to do.

Good Use of the Time

You've discovered you're in the driver's seat alone, solo. How do you begin to discover what you need to focus on? What's next? How do you make the best use of this time?

Perhaps the best advice I was ever given is this: *Don't just work on it; let it work on you.* Allow your situation to unfold naturally. Let time do its work. This requires trust. You must trust that everything happens in a certain way for a purpose and that God will work in your life in the way you need—if you allow Him to.

Another way to say it is *muddy water left alone becomes clear.* We must not poke at it, stir it, feverishly try to clean it up. Leave it alone. Sit still.

You didn't get here overnight, and the changes you must make won't happen overnight either. With your emotions swirling, you want to take action. But don't.

Again, you're looking over at the passenger seat thinking *This would be so much easier if both our hands were on the wheel.* Possibly. Possibly not. Remember, this is *your* opportunity to change, to work on yourself. You may not have another opportunity like this one. Consider it a gift given to you. This is time to drive solo, to determine *your* destination. You've been given the gift of space and time to reflect.

What might be your next step? Before you decide,

- *Consider where you are on your journey.* Using the first several chapters of this book as a launching point, reflect on how you got where you are today. What concerns have emerged? If you listen carefully, you'll know what they are. You shouldn't really need your mate to tell you anything again. It's all been said.

- *Determine to stay with your pain.* Denial tends to diminish in times of crisis; issues become crystallized. Pain has a way of making everything very clear. Now, no longer distracting yourself, you sit with the issues. Embrace your pain and ask what it's teaching you.

- *Contemplate these words of Solomon:* "If you call out for insight and cry aloud for understanding, and if you look for it as for silver and search for it as for hidden treasure, then you will understand the fear of the LORD and find the knowledge of God" (Proverbs 2:3-5). The wisdom of God is available to you.

Now consider answering the following four questions to help clarify where to start your work:

1. Has your mate complained about something over and over again?

2. What has been your typical response to this concern?

3. Is there truth in this concern?

4. What have others told you to confirm an area or areas needing growth?

Does this exercise help make things clearer? No less painful, but clearer? If so, you know what you need to do, and now you can plan your next steps.

Pace Is Critical

If you're anything like me, you want change and you want it *now*. The heck with pace. Yet impatience is not our friend.

Change doesn't work on a deadline. Even though you're in the driver's seat, directing your own life, don't try to speed through this process. If you do, you'll miss important lessons.

Okay, you've heard all that before, and you still want to rush it. I get it. I did too. But I learned the books telling me to slow down were right. The counsel telling me to take time to really learn the lessons was correct. If I had chosen to rush through this work, I probably would have come to a dead end, then had to do the work again.

So will you slow down and do the work right the first time? Or will you rush through it and have to do it again? And what do I mean by *pace*?

First and foremost, I mean moving at a speed that allows you to focus on your issues, not too fast and not too slow. You settle into a pace that feels right. If you listen to yourself, your mate, and wise counsel, you'll know how to proceed. There is no recipe for this; it just means stepping back, appreciating the lessons you must learn and changes you must make, and then setting out to do that work.

Will this process involve you participating in a 12-Step group? Will it involve individual counseling? Will you need to read and re-read certain books? What else is needed for your emotional growth? Your answer to these questions will determine the pace you need to accomplish them.

Pace also involves your mate. Remember, you're focusing primarily on yourself, but your mate remains somewhere in the picture. They have thoughts and feelings about your work, and you would do well to be attuned to that information.

Perhaps they've chosen not to assist you. Still, you must be mindful of them. Step back and consider if and how they want to interact with you. Be considerate of them, even if that doesn't mean counseling together.

All of this is dynamic, really meaning "trial and error." Because there is no recipe, you must make adjustments as you go. Trust me, you'll settle into a pace that works for you and your mate.

The Brief Break

A "brief break" is another time when you might find yourself alone in the driver's seat. Whether the break is the result of a sudden argument that erupted out of nowhere and was over nearly as soon as it started, a slow simmering struggle that hit a high spot, or a particularly spirited moment of volatility, these times of brokenness come in every marriage. Again, pace and tempo are important, as well as a determination to handle the process the best way possible.

Sometimes it's best to pull apart, allowing emotions to cool, while at other times an immediate apology and attempt to reconnect are best. Hopefully, you know your mate and are sensitive to what works best for both of you.

Take the sudden argument. You say something that triggers your mate, and they erupt. You didn't know they would erupt, otherwise you might have been more careful. But they did. How might you handle this situation?

First, *step back and assess the situation*. Did you say or do something for which you must take responsibility? Do you need to apologize for being insensitive? Have you broken your mate's heart? Step back and feel the weight of your situation.

Second, *do nothing*. As much as you want to take action, don't. Sit still. Be quiet. Allow the situation to cool and become clear. You can't think clearly if you're overwhelmed with emotion. Allow your emotions to settle. Proceed carefully. Go slowly.

Third, *do the next right thing*. If you've taken time to reflect, you'll know what the next move is, assuming there is one. You'll know what words must be spoken and what words must *not* be spoken. Again, go slowly and make moves cautiously. Do no harm. If the situation calls for an apology, offer it. Taking ownership of wrongs done with a heartfelt apology nearly always brings restoration to a difficult situation.

Third, *do your work*. Here we are again, with you being alone in the driver's seat, wishing you were in a two-way conversation. Remember, it can't always be that way. Stay focused on you. Do your reading, your journaling, your counseling, and pray. Begin to make the changes you must make. Make plans that focus on aspects of your work that are within your control.

Fourth, *calm yourself and keep things in perspective*. Remember, your feelings are your feelings, and you're responsible for them. You're responsible for soothing yourself and even healing yourself. Your mate may be a help in this process at times, while at other times you will be alone. Expect it.

Finally, *reconnect when the time is right*. It's always wonderful to reconnect when it's possible *and the time is right*, not before. When the time is right, when you're actively engaged in doing your work, your mate will often respond in kind. Reach out with the proverbial olive branch and seek peace.

Becoming More Attractive

Can a person really work on a relationship without the other? Of course. Much work done individually benefits a marriage. Don't lose sight of the fact that anything you do to make yourself a better traveling companion is indirect work on your marriage and all your relationships.

We can and should deepen some aspects of our character, and in the process, we can become more attractive to others. I share that not as a way to manipulate others but as a way to enhance your Self.

Why does anyone choose to be with us? Because we enhance their life in some way. We all have the power to evoke certain emotions in our mate. Hopefully, you're in a relationship where positive emotions are evoked more frequently than negative ones. Of course, if positive emotions are evoked, exciting the other person, attraction will occur. If not, the relationship may die.

I've found that the topic of emotional attraction is often not considered in many couples' relationships. But think about it. If you feel joy, laughter, lightheartedness, and friendship in your relationship more often than guilt and discouragement, it's likely to grow. So capitalize on positive emotions and the connection they bring.

Emotions Are Contagious

Another way to work on your marriage is to be mindful of and manage your emotional life. One of my greatest discoveries is that emotions are contagious. Well, I didn't discover this. A brilliant neuroscientist, Marco Iacoboni, discovered "mirror neurons," and their impact is astounding.

This group of neurons in the prefrontal cortex code the actions of others as well as our own. Dr. Iacoboni explained this in an interview:

> Without [these neurons], we would likely be blind to the actions, intentions and emotions of other people. The way mirror neurons likely let us understand others is by providing some kind of inner imitation of the actions of other people, which in turn leads us to "simulate" the intentions

and emotions associated with those actions. When I see
you smiling, my mirror neurons for smiling fire up, too,
initiating a cascade of neural activity that evokes the feeling we typically associate with a smile.[10]

This means I can influence your feelings and you can influence
mine. How cool is that? Of concern, of course, is the fact that my
grumpiness can influence Christie to turn away from me, becoming
grumpy herself. But if I smile broadly and offer her an outstretched
hand, chances are good she'll respond favorably.

In a recent dinner conversation with friends, we happened on the
topic of attitude. One friend, Josh, looked at another man, Jake, and
said, "You seem to be upbeat. I haven't been around you that many
times, but each time I'm with you I feel encouraged. How do you do it?"

Another friend chimed in. "I agree with Josh. Nothing seems to
keep you down long. You have your moments, to be sure, but you
always seem to bounce back. How do you do it?"

Jake didn't seem to know what to say or be sure about the observa-
tion. Still, it seemed to get him wondering.

"I guess I'm just thankful for all the blessings in my life," he said.

"C'mon, no," Josh quickly inserted. "You have a resilience about
you. How did you get that?"

Again, Jake didn't seem know what to say, but everyone at the
table looked energized by the conversation and about Jake's attitude
in particular.

"Really, I *do* feel blessed," Jake said. "I certainly have my share of
problems, and my wife can attest to my lack of resilience at times. But
I'm glad if, by and large, I give off a positive attitude."

Josh was saying he appreciated Jake's positive attitude, and he wanted
more of what his friend had. We all know emotions are contagious
because we experience it all the time. Dr. Iacoboni simply confirmed
what we've all discovered time and again. We influence the emotions
of those around us, and in turn, we're influenced by others' emotions.

What are the implications of this when we're in the marital driver's
seat alone? We evoke a certain vibe, we give off a certain attitude, and

that impacts our mate. While we can't force things to happen the way we want them to, we can control our mood and the vibe we give off. This gives us the ability and opportunity to attract our spouse.

Bridge to the Benefit

Since emotions are contagious and we're emitting positive or negative emotions all the time, it becomes even more critical to choose a positive attitude. In everything happening to you, how can you make the most of it?

Recently, I received a note from a woman who worked with me several years ago:

> Dr. Hawkins, I wanted to let you know that my time spent working with you was very helpful. While I wasn't able to save my marriage, and had a pretty rough time after we divorced, I was able to choose a positive attitude for myself. It's really true that everything is not always the way it seems at the moment. Some things I thought were negative turned out to be some of the best lessons of my life. I decided to live life to the fullest and am looking forward to my life now. Thank you again.

This woman's story isn't unique; I often receive feedback like this. Perhaps you've experienced it in your life as well—what you thought was terrible at one time turned out to be a blessing in disguise.

What if being in the driver's seat means we have a unique opportunity to look on the bright side? We've already discussed the importance of using this time for your best purposes. But what if the purpose for this time is to cultivate a positive attitude?

While it's cliché to say we should "look on the bright side," there's also powerful truth to it. There's a benefit in everything that happens to us. Managing your attitude is, after all, one of the most important things you still have complete control over.

What are some ways to cultivate a positive attitude while you're alone in the driver's seat? Here are a few things to try:

- *Keep a gratitude journal.* Whether you write out aspects of your life and keep them in a journal or simply rehearse them on a daily basis, counting your blessings is a powerful mood shifter.

- *See your situation as an opportunity for growth.* Okay, I know you didn't ask for another doggone growth opportunity, but it's landed in your lap, so you might as well make the best of it. Embrace the challenges and see what they have to teach you.

- *Find something exciting about your experience.* It isn't enough to view your situation as a challenge or opportunity. Use words that express the positives in your situation and feel the power of embracing them.

- *Live healthy.* Not enough can be said about the importance of adequate exercise, sleep, and nutrition. Also consider the importance of deep breathing. We can actually change how we feel by breathing deeply. Calm yourself by taking in deep breaths. When you do, you'll feel alive.

- *Associate with encouraging people.* We all know both encouraging and discouraging people. Some always find a reason to smile, some always find a reason to frown. Notice how you feel around people and choose which ones you want to associate with.

- *Embrace solutions to your problems.* Instead of rehearsing problems, rehearse the solutions you're putting into motion. Consider all you're doing to change your situation and feel the weight lift from your shoulders.

Practicing the above tools will help you feel better and take control of your life as well as the decisions impacting you. Choose wisely.

Seeing What You Didn't See Before

You're where you are today, and what is past cannot be changed. What you can impact is today and the future, not yesterday.

Since attitude is everything, consider embracing the attitude of seeing what you didn't see before. Traveling solo, this is what can happen without the distraction of interacting with your mate.

During the time I was apart from Christie, I heard, felt, and saw things I hadn't experienced before. It was, in a very real sense, a new beginning for me. I felt like a different man.

Perhaps the greatest gift was *time*. Not just chronological time, though that was valuable, but *kairos* time—time full of meaning and possibility. When in a sense time stood still, I was able to reflect and see things from a fresh perspective.

I discovered that when I was caught up in all my routines, I was walking through life as if on autopilot. I remember feeling surprised by how many routines I had—get up at the same time, make my lattes at the same time, start my day at the same time, end my day at the same time, go to the gym at the same time, and go to bed at the same time. I left no room to approach or experience my day differently.

And then I found myself acting a little differently—nothing earth-shattering, but different. I took myself out for dinner and tried some new dishes. I experimented again with cooking (still a disaster!) and read a novel for the first time in ten years. I went to church alone. I became comfortable with driving solo.

All of these experiences enriched my life and became the soil out of which I was growing a new me. I was able to reflect on the kind of husband I had been and the one I wanted to be. It all allowed me to see myself in a new way, preparing me to be a better man and husband.

Epiphanies

You may wonder what kind of new insights emerged from my time alone in the driver's seat, what life-changing, me-changing epiphanies came to me. I share them with you as a guide to help you in the same process.

It's not all about me. While this one should and could have come to me years earlier, the lesson circled back around. The way I view the world, the way I want the world to be, is only one way, not the *only* way.

Others offer equally valid points of view and ways to navigate through the world, and I need to consider and honor them.

I came to see how controlling I could be. I came to see how tightly I grasped onto my belongings, my money, my plans, my ways. I came to see how small my world had become because of the road map I carried with me on the path I wanted to take.

Embracing others is important. I came to see how important others were to me, starting, of course, with my wife, but expanding to my children, their mates, my grandchildren, and my friends. I didn't want to be known as the guy who works sixty-hour weeks. I wanted to be known as the guy who was fun to be around.

While it's cliché to say others are important, they really *are* important. However, it's not enough to say they're important; I must show them their importance to me. I changed the way I viewed all these important people and set out to be fully present with them.

Being fully present brings a full life. This was another huge shift. Instead of coasting through life, I decided to experience it. I want to see new sights, listen to new music, laugh, and enjoy life. This time on earth is not, as they say, a practice round. It's our one real life happening right now.

So I go to more concerts. I enjoy more meals fully. I'm present to whatever comes before me. And I travel in such a way that different experiences will come to me.

I can see God in the details. Finally, I changed my attitude about God—again. Instead of seeing Him as a "God in a box" to whom I pray, hoping beyond hope for good things, I look for Him in the small details of life. I look for His hand in the answers that come and the questions that linger. No more "easy" God.

These are a few of the "aha" moments for me. How about you? What are you learning as you drive solo?

Becoming a Better Travel Companion

I wish I could tell you who are driving solo that everything will work out beautifully. But that may be only partly true. Everything will work out beautifully if you do your work, though even then, you can't know it will for sure.

Still, you have the opportunity to grow, to be a fantastic traveling companion, and to learn the lessons you and your mate hoped you would learn. If you do this well, you may have a chance at "two hands on the wheel" again, with you taking a more active role in the direction of the relationship.

Regardless of the outcome, you're learning how to be in the driver's seat, and that's the most powerful lesson. You're learning how to take control of your life and stop trying to manage what isn't yours to manage. What you make of the opportunity is under your control. You control you and your life while your mate controls theirs.

Remember, fully appreciating who your mate is and their right to choose their own path is critical. Your task is to work on yourself so you're the best traveling companion possible and, in the process, enhance the likelihood that your mate will want to ride through life with you.

Note a few other considerations in planning for possible reconciliation. The most important consideration concerns *timing*. As I've tried to illustrate throughout this chapter, nothing should be rushed. Everything must unfold in its perfect time. If you try to force progress, your effort will backfire on you. Attempts at manipulation and control are felt as oppressive and will certainly work against you.

As you work on yourself, making yourself the most attractive person you're capable of being, you will attract others. Allow your mate the space and time to fully choose you, not to be guilt-induced into accepting you. Waiting for them to choose you will be critical, and the results will be so much more beautiful.

Do your work, and you give everything a chance to fall into place.

And So, What About Love?

Love drew your mate to you originally, and the seeds of that connection are still there. But bad habits and patterns got in the way, and now it's time to clean up some of that debris, creating opportunities to travel well together again.

For now, you may be traveling alone, but you can have a new attitude about being in the driver's seat. You now have an incredible opportunity to work on yourself. Don't squander it. Use it to become the best traveling companion possible.

Now let's explore the power and importance of listening.

7

TURN DOWN THE RADIO...
AND LISTEN TO ME

Becoming a Better Listener

*If we can share our story with someone who responds with
empathy and understanding, shame can't survive.*

BRENÉ BROWN

We discovered a fantastic radio station while vacationing on Cape Cod—91.1 on the dial, as I recall. We spent the entire week traveling around the Cape listening to an engaging DJ talking about and playing old pop music. It was entertaining, and I decided to find a station like it when I got back home.

So today, as soon as I got into my car, I began searching for the perfect radio station, like the one I heard on Cape Cod. I grabbed the tuning knob and began a slow and somewhat painful process. I moved from clear reception (but the wrong station) to scratchy sounds and then back to clear stations (still the wrong ones). Twenty minutes later I gave up, the scratchy whirring too much to take.

My twenty minutes of struggle seeking clear music reminded me of the challenges we have in really hearing each other. Does it ever seem to you that many of us are speaking on a different frequency than our mate is hearing—or vice versa? Someone is speaking, to be sure, and someone may be trying to listen, but we're not tuned in to each other. The result is noise and tension.

As you travel on this journey with your mate, it's critical to be tuned in and listen—and that is what this chapter is about. After all, listening is *the* way we connect. Listening is *the* bridge between people, connecting ideas, feelings, moods, and, ultimately, a sense of shared direction. Connection is what we seek as we journey with a mate, what this whole book is about.

Remember, you could have chosen to travel alone, but you chose one person in particular to ride with you. Picking them out of a crowd, you imagined this companion and the journey you were taking together would come with adventure, full of twists and turns, hills and valleys, wanted and unwanted surprises—and you *still* chose them.

This person is an individual, not an extension of you. Sometimes we forget this truth, slipping into believing our mate should want what we want and do what we want to do. They should speak in a way that makes it easy for us to listen, following all our expectations.

But they're different, and it's our responsibility to fully attend to them. This means listening well. As much as you might think you know about listening—and most of us know a thing or two—we can always learn more and practice with new tools to get better.

Listening and being heard is the focus of this chapter—turning down the radio, adjusting the frequency for clarity, and offering our mate our undivided attention. Unfortunately, many of us have to be reminded to do that. We have to be asked to listen when really this should be a natural part of caring about others. We insist our mate look at us and give us their full attention.

To really be together, to be really connected, we must listen well. We must acknowledge our mates, who are always different from us with different values, preferences, quirks, and delights. That's part of the reason we chose to travel with them. They are worthy of being valued, respected, and listened to.

Traveling Cape Cod

Before our week on Cape Cod, I had forgotten about the meandering roads of the Cape. Fortunately, we weren't on any time schedule, so we often just went where the road took us—which is, in some respects, much like life. We came to appreciate the surprises around every corner—again, much like life.

Our plans were dynamic, open to change. Sentiments changed, preferences changed, and itineraries changed. This is partly what makes travel so much fun; it's unpredictable. But listening amid change becomes all the more critical. You have to be sensitive, tuned in to your travel partner.

"Where should we go today?" I asked Christie.

"Let's head toward Yarmouth," she answered, aware this was a dynamic plan, open for ambling about.

We headed for Yarmouth, but several thrift shops and coffee shops later, we were still some distance from our intended destination. That was okay, however, since we had the luxury of time and the inclination to appreciate the journey. Again, listening to each other was key, even in a relaxed mode of traveling.

After a couple of hours of driving, we were ready for lunch.

"I remember a quaint inn down the road," I said. "Do you remember it?"

"Vaguely. Was it the one connected to the bed and breakfast in South Yarmouth?"

"I think so." Talking to each other, sharing ideas, made travel so enjoyable. This is the way communication can be. This is the way it must be if we're going to stay connected.

Tuning In

Much has been written about the skill and art of listening. Even with the abundance of information about it, we still do rather poorly when it comes to truly hearing one another, *really tuning in*. Why is that?

Listening requires us to fully attend to others. We're often so filled with our own ideas that we have little room left for someone else. To really listen to others, we must "turn down the radio," meaning, we must rid ourselves of distractions.

We often believe listening is easy—simply look at the other person and listen to what they're saying. But it's really much more difficult than that. Listening is hard work—like traveling with another person who sees the world differently from you with different ideas, beliefs, values, and preferences.

Listening is hard work because this other individual may not always agree with you. They may insist on something you find disagreeable. Still, attending to them and listening despite those differences is *the* way to connect, to really tune in and solve any problems that might arise.

When we fully grasp this truth—that listening is difficult and takes focus and deliberate attention—we've already begun to solve the problem. Listening is not always easy, and we shouldn't expect it to be so. Like finding a clear frequency on the radio, *tuning in* can be challenging.

This is why much has been expressed about *active listening*, where you're a fully engaged and active participant, as opposed to *passive listening*, where you're not fully engaged. In active listening, you're fully engaged, asking questions, checking out perceptions, adding to the conversation. You're very much a part of what is being said and what is being processed. In passive listening, you simply listen to what is being said.

In our marriage journey, where we're striving for connection, there is no room for passivity. We must always be engaged to remain connected.

It is tempting (because it's work) to forget the task before us and slip into passive listening. We become lazy. It's easy to become complacent and disengage, letting the speaker do all the work.

"Please listen" sounds like a simple enough request, but it's not. We want the listener to not only hear our words but care about them. We want the listener to be engaged, empathizing with us and validating our experience. Simply hearing the words of another may not be so hard, but active listening is another matter.

Here are a few of the challenges to active listening, to *tuning in*.

We're often distracted. When we're talking with someone, often more than one thing is happening—music playing, a television droning in the background, or others speaking nearby—and concentrating on listening and tuning in can be challenging. Rarely are we in an ideal atmosphere to hear and be heard.

Remember that some of this distraction is natural. For example, it's natural to be distracted when multiple people are talking. Screening out multiple conversations is challenging.

At any point in time, we may also be lost in our own world. We react to something someone said, setting off a cascade of thoughts. The critical issue is choosing when and how to rejoin the conversation, perhaps even sharing with them where we've been and what we've been thinking about. Including them in our world, and joining them in theirs, is what we're after.

We have feelings about the communicator. As shallow as this sounds, we may be challenged by our feelings about the communicator. If we don't like them, for whatever reason, listening will be that much harder. If we have unfinished business with them, such as resentment or anger, listening will be even more of a challenge. We must then manage those feelings to truly hear what's being said.

Can you hear the importance of caring about the communication? Listening, especially when we have distracting thoughts and feelings, is a matter of respect. Listening to someone is a way to show respect and indicate they have value.

We aren't really interested in the topic. How can we listen well if we don't care about the topic? We can feign interest, but that doesn't usually work. The task, again, is to stir up genuine interest, whenever possible, so we can attend meaningfully. We can discover something of interest in everyone.

Christie has this down to an art form—seriously. She seems to consistently find interest in others' stories and lives, even when they appear quite disparate from her own.

During our trip to Cape Cod, she struck up a conversation with the couple sitting next to us at dinner. There was nothing obvious to create a bridge between us—they were just a couple enjoying dinner together. But Christie began asking questions. First came the easy ones about where they were from and how they ended up on the Cape. That led to talking about their primary residence in Florida, where Christie has spent time.

Can you see how, with a bit of ingenuity and care, she finds ways to connect? She discovers commonalities and connections, which is exciting and energizing.

We lack empathy. The importance here is that we may be listening to the facts of the matter but not hearing how the other person is feeling— meaning we don't really imagine being in the speaker's shoes, which is a critical component to active listening.

With a bit of effort and genuine interest, we *can* feel empathy for others. We *can* discover bits and pieces of another person's story that connect to our own. We really do have only a certain number of degrees of separation between us, and those degrees can be minimized with just a touch of effort.

We make judgments. It's tempting to make rash judgments about what the person we're listening to is saying, closing off any possible connection to them. If we deem what they're saying as wrong or shallow, or make some other negative judgment, we've stopped truly listening.

At a family gathering recently, my nephew shared about having a pet pig. A pet pig! I was aware of being judgmental, thinking no one should have a pet pig. Then, partly because I really like Matthew, I took an interest in this topic. What was it like to have a pet pig in his house? Suddenly, a new world opened up to me, and my connection to him was strengthened as he enjoyed sharing stories about his growing farm life.

When we care about people, they open up to us. When we show an interest in their story, they share more and become more human to us. Then they, in turn, show an interest in our life, creating connection. Judgment recedes, and in its place comes caring, concern, and connection.

We have a closed mind. Finally, all these factors lead to a closed mind. At some level, and for whatever reason, we decide not to really listen to this person. So we hear their words, but we don't allow their words to penetrate.

People can, of course, sense when we're critical of their life choices. They know when we disapprove of their decisions as opposed to finding their lives interesting. We have a short time to convey either openness and receptivity or a disapproving closed attitude.

The solution, if we seek connection, is to actively listen and take an interest in others. This is such a powerful truth, and it forms the basis for connection. People know when we care, and when they do, they share their story with us. Their story weaves its way into our story, and this is incredibly energizing. We create connections to others by hearing their stories and then bringing ours to the conversation.

Being Fully Present

Before becoming fast friends with the couple from Florida at dinner, we couldn't help but notice tension building between them as the woman played with her phone, answering and sending texts. Her husband became noticeably more annoyed.

"Will you please put that phone down?" he finally blurted.

She looked up and said something, but she didn't stop texting.

Here was another situation that needed "turning down the radio." The husband tried to get his wife to be fully present with him, but she was caught up in a world that didn't include him.

I must admit, Christie has asked me to turn off my phone at dinner in the past. In retrospect, it seems so obvious that I needed to do that to show her respect, but at the time my phone seemed so important.

The man sitting next to us obviously felt annoyed and disrespected. He was being ignored while his wife was having conversations with other people who weren't at the table with them. She missed an opportunity for connection with her husband.

Being fully present is challenging but necessary for connection. Caring about who you're with and letting them know they're the most important person in your world at that moment is what active listening is all about.

Allowing Ourselves
to Be Influenced

Being fully present is perhaps the most important building block to listening. We can't listen well if we're not fully present and available. Remember, hearing each other creates connection. This is all about conveying to your partner that they're the most important person in your world at that moment. All distractions are put aside, and full attention is given to your spouse.

What would have happened if, when the husband asked his wife to put her phone away, she replied, "I'm sorry for being distracted. I want to be with you."

Let's imagine, spicing up my story, that she then grabs his hand, looks into his eyes, and says, "I'm glad to be out to dinner with you. Isn't this a lovely place?"

Farfetched? No. He made an awkward bid for his wife's attention and, indirectly to be sure, let her know he was feeling ignored. She rebuffed him, missing an opportunity for connection. But she could have changed course.

We all have these kinds of situations where our mate tries to connect with us, and we have an opportunity to respond favorably. See how important listening can be? When we receive a signal as we journey together, we must respond to the need/request of the moment. If we respond favorably, we make connection. If we miss the opportunity, we create disconnection.

Can you see this?

When I keep my phone on during dinner, I send a signal to my wife and the rest of the world that I'm unavailable. I'm not fully present.

Being open to being influenced by our mate, hearing and seeing the request for connection, is no small matter. It means being flexible. We diminish distractions, look at our spouse, stay focused on them, and seek to fully understand what they're saying to us. What they say is important and worthy of our full attention. Their words are an effort to connect, and we must decide what we will do with them.

Sam

Seeking to understand another person means believing they have something important to say to us. It means creating enough space within ourselves so we hear them. We listen for their requests, their concerns for attention.

Have you ever had a conversation with someone when all you could think was, *They're not listening to me!* They were like stoic, unemotional Spock from *Star Trek*, your words bouncing off them, you speaking as though into thin air.

Connection broken. Opportunity missed.

I had a counseling session recently with a man whose mind-set seemed impenetrable. He was there under protest, referred by his wife. Fifty years old and separated from her, he came in angry and left just as angry, my nudging making little impact. He came with that impenetrable mind-set, and he left with the same one.

I sensed things might not go well after his first words.

"I'm here only because of my wife," he said, frowning. "She made me come. She said if I didn't change, she was done with our marriage. But she's got just as much to change as I do."

Sam's anger was palpable, his sarcastic attitude immediately apparent. While his words challenged me to talk him out of his position, I knew that would be impossible. So rather than accept his challenge, I tried to hear the pain beneath his anger.

"She controls everything in my life," he said. "Now she's even telling me I have to be in counseling, and she'll divorce me if I don't change. That is not okay."

"Why is she pushing for counseling, Sam?" I asked. "Let's talk about her pain."

"I'm really tired of hearing about her pain. She says I don't listen to her. I do listen. She doesn't listen to me."

I paused for a moment. Sam certainly felt controlled, and his attitude was getting in the way of working effectively with his wife. His anger and feelings of powerlessness created a barrier to hearing her cry for help.

"Tell me some more about your marriage and what led to your separation. I imagine this has been hard on you."

"We've separated a bunch of times. Which one do you want me to talk about?"

"How about this one?"

"We've been separated for six months this time. She says I'm angry. You bet I'm angry. She kicked me out. Wouldn't you be angry? She's got just as big a part in this as I do."

"What is her part in this, do you think?"

"Separating from me, for starters. We're married, after all. Separation always leads to divorce, and this shows she's really not invested in our marriage. If she doesn't care about me, I'm not going to care about her."

"Whoa," I said. "I'm concerned with how you're thinking about this. Is it possible she actually *did* need to separate to get your attention, to get you to really tune in to her feelings? I know it's drastic, but maybe that's what actually did need to happen."

"No way!" he said. "Kicking me out? I want to be in my home with my wife, but she won't have me back unless I change, and I'm not going to change until she asks me to come back home."

"Sounds like a vicious cycle. If you won't change until she lets you back home, and she won't ask you to come back home because you're unwilling to change, doesn't that leave you in a tough place?"

"Welcome to my world," he said sarcastically.

"Seems like what we might do, Sam, is really look at what your wife has been trying to say to you. Let's tune in to her message and give her a sensitive response to it."

"I'm hearing her just fine. When is she going to listen to me? I'm tired of listening to her."

"I can hear that. But I think you will have to listen to her first, and at some point, she'll be able to hear you. But not now."

Sam paused, and I thought for a moment he might make an emotional turn. He didn't, and in fact, he grew angrier.

"She's just as much at fault as I am," he continued, hitting his fist on the chair. "I'm really tired of being pushed around by her. I'm not going to be the only one working on this. I think I'm done with her. I'll talk to you later—maybe."

With that, he got up and stomped out of my office. Sam was stuck. He was angry and rigid in his thinking. Unless he shifts and learns to hear his wife's concerns, this separation will continue and possibly lead to divorce, an outcome Sam doesn't want. He has work to do if he wants to save his marriage. He needs to become more vulnerable, delve into his hurt, and understand how his anger and behavior impact his wife. Neither is listening to the other well, and this has to change if they're to save their marriage.

Listening with Vulnerability

Sam is ready for battle. Can you see how defensive he is? He has layers and layers of protection to avoid risk of vulnerability, and the result is distance and detachment.

Sam is behaving a bit like all of us do when we're filled with hurt and pain. He's protecting himself, and in his case, he's doing it with anger and sarcasm. All he hears are the voices in his head telling him how wronged he's been, while his wife's voice and pain recede into the background.

Sam rehearses his pain. He thinks it all comes from his wife's actions, when in fact, much of his pain has to do with his behavior making matters worse. He needs to take off a few layers of protection, preparing instead for nakedness, exposure, vulnerability. Not literally naked, of course, but in a manner of speaking. The fewer layers of protection he has, the better. The more vulnerable and exposed he is, the better his chances of connecting to his wife.

Sam needs to tune in to his wife, find her frequency, speak her language, reflect her message, and let her words impact him. He needs to be fully present, ready to change. Adapting this attitude will likely reach and impact his mate.

While we don't know exactly what Sam's wife is thinking, we can imagine she feels unheard and exasperated. She sees and feels an angry man, defending himself against being vulnerable with her. She doesn't feel connected to him. She isn't feeling drawn to him.

How might she respond if Sam dropped his angry guard, tuned in to her, and exposed his vulnerability to her? Sam keeps digging himself in deeper with his angry demeanor, and he's become angrier over time, not less angry. He's covered his sadness and fear with anger, and in the process, he misses his wife's attempts to reach him, to be heard and valued.

Why is Sam really so angry? Because exposing his fear and sadness is uncomfortable for him. Truly listening, however, poses a risk. Listening to information he may not want to hear could be difficult, even painful, and his anger is protecting him. Sam is, in a sense, living in his own protective world, free from feeling vulnerable to his wife.

The Risk and Benefit of Vulnerability

If Sam truly listens to what his wife is saying, he will need to consider her words and perceptions. He must confront his denial, which will leave him feeling vulnerable. The risk of really listening is *vulnerability*.

How does it feel when we allow ourselves to be vulnerable?

While we may say we want to listen and be vulnerable, few of us actually choose this aspect of relating. This level of connection can be frightening. Vulnerability means exposing ourselves, sharing our truest feelings and thoughts. It means putting ourselves out there so others know exactly what we think, feel, and believe.

More often we hide and protect ourselves. We share as little of ourselves as possible so we won't feel vulnerable and exposed. We defend ourselves and guard against appearing or feeling weak.

Sam conveyed a bravado that hid more vulnerable feelings. His blaming and attacking covered the vulnerability he felt in relationship to his wife. I suspect he felt frightened and out of control when it came to her, and he needed to be able to talk about those feelings.

In her book *Daring Greatly*, Brené Brown brings greater awareness to the topic of vulnerability, defining it as "uncertainty, risk, and emotional exposure." She also states that "vulnerability is the birthplace of love, belonging, joy, courage, empathy and creativity."[11]

This is a beautiful description of vulnerability. When we show up vulnerably, we do risk feeling uncertain, even anxious. We can never be sure how we will be perceived and treated. But we will have been present and have opened the opportunity for real connection.

Sam is undoubtedly feeling exposed, his wife's criticisms looming large in his mind. Sam acts tough as a way to guard against feeling the weight of her criticism and his subsequent hurt, weakness, and uncertainty. His defenses against vulnerability—to be angry, tough, and resolved—only exacerbate his problems, of course. Fighting against his wife only aggravates his problems and their problems. Listening fully would mean feeling even more vulnerable. Yet this is his only path to change and reconnection.

True listening means being vulnerable, exposing our insecure, frightened selves. If we allow ourselves to be fully impacted by another person, if we allow their words to settle into us, we must be vulnerable to them and their words.

In her article "Emotional Vulnerability as the Path to Connection," Dr. Dianne Grande says if we really want to connect, we must expose our real selves to one another. This takes listening and being listened to.

Grande says this about emotional vulnerability:

> You've decided to partner with someone, and you begin to feel the fear that this person will get to know you better than you know yourself. These situations are more frightening to some of us than to others, depending upon our personal histories, our cultural backgrounds, and our basic personality traits.[12]

Was Sam afraid of allowing his wife to fully know him? Did he fear feeling shame at the risk of fully listening to her?

What about you and me? What are the risks of really listening, taking in what our mate has to say about us? What are the risks of having real, meaningful conversations with the person we married? These risks cause significant anxiety if we don't know ourselves or we don't feel securely attached to our mate. Real connection can be like walking around naked, and that's scary. However, only by allowing ourselves to be vulnerable can we feel love and true connection. By being vulnerable, we allow ourselves to be seen and loved.

Empathy

Listening fully in my marriage, with my heart as well as my head, means hearing what Christie has to say. It means getting out of my own emotional space and into hers. This is the heart of empathy.

Empathy in marriage, remember, is the ability to feel what our mate feels and see the world through their eyes. This can occur only with active listening. We must take a keen interest in their world, ask gentle questions, and consider what they're saying.

Let's explore in more depth how you might build empathy into your marriage.

Become aware of your own emotions. While this may seem counter-intuitive, since we're learning how to focus on someone else, we must be aware of our own feelings to be able to relate to their feelings. After all, empathy is relating to another person's experience.

Tune in to your mate's emotions. Active listening involves hearing the emotions behind the story your mate is telling you. Are they excited about something happening to them? Are they sad about a loss in their life? What exactly are they feeling and how might you best resonate with those feelings?

Consider the need behind your mate's story. People are often sharing a need embedded in their story. Perhaps your mate simply needs you to listen, but sometimes they need more than that. Tune in to the need they might be expressing and interact with them on that basis.

Imagine what it's like for your mate as they share. As your spouse shares their story, imagine what it's like for them. You can even say, "I imagine you…" Or, "Knowing you, I can imagine…" These are ways to not only empathize but to show them you're listening and trying to experience what they're experiencing.

Extend a perception check. Finally, tell them what you believe they're experiencing, and then ask if you're correct. Your mate will tell you if you've understood, and they might even share more information with you.

Practicing these empathy skills is a great way to listen fully to your mate. These skills will help you stay focused on your spouse and let them know you're listening.

Being Influenced

The whole point of active listening is being willing to experience active connection. Being in relationship means being open to being influenced by your mate, growing in the process.

Listening fully, being fully present, means risking hearing how others are different from us. It means caring about their different backgrounds, how they've come from a different culture and perhaps have different political and faith experiences. By virtue of being different, they can be interesting to us, expanding who we are. Listening fully means being open to changing.

Back to Sam, he's created a closed system, rigidly attaching himself to his beliefs. He's made up his mind about his wife, and fueled by resentment and bitterness, he rehearses how wronged he feels. He's not particularly open to seeing life from any vantage point that contradicts his own. He can't see how this myopic rigidity keeps him at arm's length from his wife. Sadly, he's not open to being influenced by her. Is it any wonder that she feels unheard and pushes away?

Sam returned, and now I'm working with him to help him see that he's his own worst enemy. His wife is not his enemy, and the more he rehearses her being his enemy, the more stuck he is. His path back to her is not simply being open to listening to her but recognizing how sad and hurt he is beneath his protective anger. Vulnerability, remember, is the pathway to connection for all of us, including Sam. Learning to listen to what his wife has been trying to say will create connection if he's willing to do that work.

Honesty and Criticism

A central aspect of vulnerability and active listening involves hearing things we would much rather not hear. Being closed—hearing only our own thoughts, values, and preferences—has its advantages. But being closed is not possible in a real relationship.

True listening, tuning in to another person, sometimes involves hearing criticism, which under the best of circumstances can be challenging. Let's explore the issue of criticism and how we can best navigate this slippery, winding path.

Criticism, feedback that suggests we're doing something not beneficial and useful, is part and parcel of every relationship. Failing to create a climate where criticism can be freely given means partners tiptoe around each other, guarding what they say, creating even more distance and distrust.

The answer to real connection involves creating an atmosphere where you can receive, as well as offer, criticism. This is not a time to tell your mate what's wrong with them. That's a character attack. It's a time to provide useful feedback, leading to necessary change.

Here are five strategies you can build into your relationship to help both you and your mate give and receive critical feedback:

1. *Determine the goal of the feedback.* Is this feedback really necessary? Is it truly given for the betterment of the marriage? Many times we share "feedback" to get something off our chest that would be better off not said. Make the goal of your feedback clear from the start, such as "I want to spend more time with you. Will you free up some evenings so we can have time together?"

2. *Choose the right time to share information. Never* offer criticism during a fight. This is not an opportunity to prove a point or shame your mate. Criticism is meant to be useful, helpful feedback. "I'm frightened by your driving, and I'm asking you to please slow down."

3. *Share a specific situation and your feelings about it.*

Remember, you're offering information, and you want your mate to know how something they do impacts you. Be clear that your reaction is your reaction and that you own it. You might say, "I'm uncomfortable with your parents, and I would prefer to spend less time with them during the holidays. I want to hear your preferences and what's important to you too."

4. *Align your criticism with your mate's goals.* Remember, this information can be useful, and you need to show your mate *how* it can be helpful to them. Show how this information will enhance your connection. "If we can agree on how to spend the holidays, we'll both enjoy them and our families a lot more."

5. *Maintain a positive connection.* Remember the old adage "No one cares what you think unless they think you care." Bear this in mind as you share the information. Find ways to put a positive spin on it and remind your mate you truly care about them.

These tools are just that—tools. Nothing makes giving or receiving criticism easy. However, as you practice giving and receiving criticism, creating safety and compassion, your relationship has the opportunity to grow.

But I Hate Critical Feedback!

After reading these best ways to give critical feedback, some of you have got to be thinking, along with me, *But I hate critical feedback! I don't care if I grow.*

Yes, I'm with you. Denial and I have gotten along fine for many years. The second I start to hear something critical, my heart begins to race, my pulse speeds up, and my thoughts are flooded with explanations and defenses. I'm not proud of my reaction, but that's the truth of the matter. I'm not always a huge fan of emotional growth.

What can we do to lessen our harsh reaction to receiving criticism from our mate? Here are a few things I'm working on myself:

Slow down your first reaction. In other words, don't react. Stop yourself from blurting out some explanation for your actions. Just slow everything down so you can think about what's being said.

Then listen. Really listen. What is at the heart of what's being said? What is the message your spouse is giving you? As you listen for the heart of the matter, you'll create some time to truly consider the message. Calm and still, you'll have a much better chance of really hearing them.

Listen for understanding. Your mate wants to know you care about what they're saying and why they're saying it. As you reflect your understanding, your mate will feel heard. Also, as you listen for understanding, catching the deeper meaning of your mate's message, you truly connect with them instead of being wrapped up in your own feelings.

Ask questions to fully appreciate the message. Again, take your time, breathe, and listen, but then ask questions to ensure you fully understand the problem. This will help dissolve some or perhaps all your panic. You're okay, and this situation will get resolved.

Address the problem. Take ownership of the issue and vow to make necessary changes. Feel appropriate guilt if you've done something wrong, but don't slip into shame. Guilt is an appropriate response to wrongdoing; shame—a feeling of being inadequate and failing—is a deeper issue that may need to be addressed at another time, in another way. Reassure your mate you've heard them and won't make that mistake again.

Follow up with your mate later. Don't be satisfied to move quickly beyond the situation. Your task is to face the current issue, ensure you tune in to your mate, and rectify the problem. Make arrangements to follow up with your mate later to ensure they're satisfied with your resolution to change.

That's not so bad, is it? We can do this, one step at a time.

Responding Authentically

Any relationship must be grounded in authenticity—being real with each other. Being real means we might look at our mate and say something like, "I'm trying hard to listen and be fully present," or "I'm doing the best I can, and I'll keep trying," or even "I'm struggling not to defend myself. I really want you to be heard, and I really want to hear you."

Now, these responses are admittedly clunky, but authentic relating *is* clunky at times.

Additionally, being authentic looks different in our different relationships. Not all relationships are as real as other ones. We decide how real we're going to be, and the quality and depth of a relationship will be equal to the degree to which we're real with each other.

I remember the moment my friend Lee said these words to me: "David, do you trust me?"

My stomach clenched as I braced myself for feedback. I knew he was going to say some hard things, and I had a moment to decide if I wanted to hear them. I could have said, "No, Lee. I actually don't trust you," or perhaps, "Yes, but I'm not open for any critical feedback, thanks."

But I said yes, and he proceeded to be authentic with me.

"David," he began, "you're too full of yourself at times. You think too much of what you believe, leaving others little room to be themselves with you."

Wow, he went straight to the heart of the matter.

We spent the next twenty minutes talking about this issue in my life and the challenges my attitude had made for me and those I care about. He was right, and I thanked him for his authentic feedback. He thanked me in turn for my willingness to hear him.

Real relationships are real at times. If we're going to be vulnerable and honest with each other in marriage, we take risks. Risks for authentic relating.

Focused Attention

Listening is as much an art as it is a skill, and it must be practiced, time and again.

I practice listening to Christie. I work at it. Listening doesn't always come easily or naturally to me, and sometimes I feel like a preschooler learning the alphabet.

I have to practice caring about what my wife cares about, because at times that just doesn't come naturally either. Some of her interests are a stretch for me, but I *want* to care about what she cares about, so that's my starting place.

What I've found most useful is *focused attention*. This involves me clearing out space in my brain for Christie. This means keeping my phone off during dinner. It means setting aside time and space to conduct my work, keeping good boundaries so that when I'm with her, *I'm with her*. It's an emotional/mental thing. Multitasking is distracting and doesn't lend itself to being present.

I've discovered I tend to care about what I attend to, and vice versa. I've found that I can positively impact my caring. In other words, I can *learn* to care. When we take a genuine interest in something, the focus of our attention naturally becomes more interesting to us.

Another way of saying this is that we can find nearly anything interesting. A case in point was at that same dinner on Cape Cod. I noticed the busboy did a wonderful job of clearing and resetting the table next to us, and I decided to compliment him. This led to Christie asking him how long he'd worked there, about his plans for the fall, and about some other aspects of his life. It was an interesting conversation. His life was interesting.

What's remarkable is that some time back I might have been annoyed at this conversation and its delaying our plans. This time, however, I took an interest in this young man. We really had no place we had to be, and this conversation was lively. Christie enjoyed herself, and I did too—all because we chose to listen, take an interest, and attend to someone.

People love being noticed. People love talking about themselves. People love being heard. So does your mate.

Waiting for the Story

I've heard it said that the opposite of talking isn't listening. It's waiting—attentive waiting. It's allowing time before you speak, making sure you've fully heard the person, allowing their story to unfold.

In some cultures, the point of sharing is to build on the story someone else is sharing. In other words, the conversation isn't simply conveying thoughts but *building a story*. Everyone in the conversation adds something to the story, and so the story grows and grows until it's naturally complete.

Isn't that fascinating?

What if we approached our conversations as if they were some kind of story? We listen not only to the words but pay attention to the underlying emotion, any concerns embedded in the words, and the direction the conversation seems to be taking. Doesn't this sound engaging? Not only might we listen differently if we listened for the story, but we might participate more fully. We might share in the story being told. We'd become active players in this unfolding drama.

This approach to conversation makes it a bit like a game, like one I play with my granddaughter, Maisie. She starts a story with only a word. Then I add a word, then she adds a word, and so on. Sometimes the story is funny, sometimes a bit dramatic. But it's always a story. Perhaps this story-like quality is something we need to add to our conversations.

And So, What About Love?

Again, the feeling of love is important. It's the foundation to any marital relationship. It's the place where the journey begins. We must have that feeling. But we need more. Traveling well together means listening is something more we can all bring to our marriage.

Someone has said giving our attention to someone, really tuning in to them, is the highest form of love. Paying attention to our mate's words, their story, is the greatest honor we can give them. Participating with them in their story is an even grander gesture, and we can both grow in the process.

Let's move forward once more, this time to explore the power and importance of staying in our own lane.

8

STAYING IN YOUR OWN LANE

The Importance and Power of Boundaries

think all the counsel I've ever offered could be condensed to one sentence: *Stay in your own lane.*

Of course, it's more complicated than that, but the truth captured in this phrase is enormous. If we're to have healthy relationships, we really must learn to stay in our own lane. So much emotional and relational health is wrapped up in learning whose business is whose business, and then living accordingly. And when it comes to marriage, being a good traveling companion and tending to the shift we've already talked about pertains to staying in our own lane.

I'm excited to dive into this topic—or should I say *drive* into it? If we really stayed in our own lane, paid attention to the rules of our road, and were sensitive to others nearby, we'd stay out of a lot of trouble and enjoy our ride.

While we travel through life, ideally with a special someone with whom we share handling the wheel, balancing that wheel is all-important. When do we pull a little and when do we let go? These are critical concepts. A sudden tug this way or that, and we're out of control. Traveling together requires a deft touch and a soft heart.

Still, staying in our own lane isn't as easy as it sounds. The markers in life aren't nearly as clear as the yellow lines down the middle of the road. Out on the highway we have the advantage of traffic moving in the same direction, signs telling us to slow down or speed up, and cars with lights on top to enforce it all.

In all our relationships, though, we rely on ourselves to guide us—the part of us that ideally monitors our comings and goings. If we're mindless in our actions, which is too often the case, we're even more likely to get into trouble.

This chapter will help you become more mindful as you strive to stay in your own lane, especially within your marriage. You'll soon see the importance of minding the business that is only yours and not minding your mate's.

Whose Business Is Whose?

I'm sure we can all agree that we need to mind our own business. We've been taught that since kindergarten—and for good cause. Parents and teachers know the importance of this concept. Society is largely built on it—*take care of yourself and offer others the courtesy of managing their own lives.*

We know meddling in someone else's business is a moral, ethical, and certainly relational violation. No one wants someone putting their two cents' worth in their business uninvited. Uninvited advice is always perceived as criticism. Even invited input can be difficult to hear, never mind the input offered without invitation.

But how do we determine whose business is whose? That's the million-dollar question, and not knowing how to make this determination is the source of many of our problems. How can we know when/if we've committed emotional trespassing?

These questions aren't as difficult as they might first appear. For example, if I think my friend Lee should go to the gym more often, whose business am I in? Lee's. If I worry about an earthquake hitting Seattle, whose business am I in? God's. If I worry about flooding, whose business am I in? Again, God's. These are issues over which I have no control.

Now let's turn to my wife. If I think she should wear a different type of clothing, I'm in her business (not that I can't have preferences about what colors I like best on her).

But if I worry about not spending enough time practicing piano, I'm finally in my own business. This is something I can control and that belongs to me. It's my business and, frankly, no one else's. When I'm in my business, I'm in an arena where I can have an impact. In fact, I'm empowered because all my energies are being directed toward something over which I have some measure of control.

Can you see the patterns here? When I'm in someone else's business, not only do I have no control over a particular issue and how that person deals with it, but I'm committing emotional trespassing. I'm in their business, where I don't belong.

Additionally, when I'm in someone else's business, they're likely to feel violated. While they may not say as much, they will *feel* it and likely react in some way. They may push back, push away, retreat.

So learning whose business is whose is a foundational principle to healthily relating to everyone and to traveling well with our mate.

Boundary Lines

This matter of whose business is whose gets murky; the boundary lines are not always clear, and they're rarely marked. I often wish they were clearer. I often wish for emotional boundaries like physical ones. And newer cars are now equipped with buzzers that sound if you cross the center line of the road. You know immediately if you've strayed out of your own lane, allowing you to make real-time adjustments. Relational boundaries are not so clear and distinct.

I remember my parents making this point when I was small: "If it doesn't belong to you, leave it alone." The guideline here is clear. If the object of my desire isn't mine, I need to leave it alone. If it has some-one else's name on it, I need to leave it alone.

While my parents' advice was helpful, it didn't settle matters in my own mind as to how best to attend to whose business was whose. What if I really wanted to play with that particular toy even if it wasn't mine? No alarm would sound if I played with it, and most often, no one was close by to police use of the toy. So the only guard over the situation was my conscience—and you can guess what I did with that. If the object was more desirable than the power of my conscience, desire won out.

In much of life, thankfully, the boundary lines are clearer. My car belongs to me, and it's locked when not in my use. My home belongs to me, and it's locked when I'm not around. Most people understand these boundary lines and respect them, if not because of the locks then because of the policing occurring around these issues. Taking a car or breaking into a home is a crime with severe punishment, so we honor these boundaries.

But what about emotional and relational boundaries? As I said, they don't exist in a literal sense. I have no locks on my emotions, no stripes on the highway of my thoughts and feelings to warn someone to keep out. We must learn emotional boundaries, and, unfortunately, most of us have never received good instruction when it comes to them.

Still, like our personal homes, cars, and belongings, our emotional and thought life are personal. Our opinions and thoughts belong to us. Our values belong to us, as do our preferences. These are all deeply personal, and we can, and must, inform those in our world about them. We can learn soon enough about how others are going to treat our personal boundaries and if they will care for them in such a way that we feel safe.

Traveling on the highway of marriage, then, depends on us cultivating clear boundaries, identifying our lane, and determining if our traveling companion will honor them.

Teaching Others How to Treat Us

Without literal lines or police to enforce emotional boundaries, it becomes imperative that we take responsibility for teaching others how to treat us. We must understand and accept this is our task—no one will do this for us, nor should they.

This is a profoundly important concept, perhaps especially for marriage, and I want to make sure you understand it. *We teach people how to treat us.* This means that others, for the most part, can and will learn how we expect to be treated. And if we're consistent and clear, reinforcing the boundaries important to us, they will honor them.

Please understand there will always be people who are boundary-breakers, and we'll explore how to best deal with them. For now, however, it's important to recognize we're responsible for being clear and consistent when it comes to our personal boundaries.

Early in our dating life, Christie said to me, "Please don't tease me. I find it hurtful, and I don't like it."

I couldn't believe what she was saying. Having grown up with four siblings and forty kids on our block, where teasing was part of the social norm, what she said sounded incredibly foreign to me, almost like a foreign language.

I couldn't understand this.

"But teasing is good-natured," I said, insistent. "It's a way to have fun."

"It's not fun for me. Teasing is at someone else's expense, and I don't like it. People get hurt by it. Please don't do it. If you continue to do it, I'm going to pull away from you."

Whose business is it if Christie doesn't want to be teased? Hers, clearly. I had little choice but to honor it, and because I care about her and her feelings, I've worked hard to honor her request. She drew a boundary and informed me how she preferred to be treated. She was prepared to police her boundary, and so I was even more inclined to respect her wishes.

Christie's lesson was important in our relationship for many reasons. Let's look closely at what she did and the impact it had on me and others in her life.

She clarified her boundary. Christie has been perfectly clear about where she stands on teasing. She knows she doesn't like it, and she's made it clear she won't tolerate it. Since it's her business, and she has the power to enforce it, this boundary works for her.

She honored her feelings that influenced her boundary. Understanding our feelings is critical because they give us important information about what's important to us. Our feelings point us in the direction we need to go in setting boundaries. Our feelings also inform others about the importance of those boundaries to us and the impact any violation is likely to have on the relationship.

She gave herself permission to have and set this boundary. Christie won't tolerate teasing in her relationships, and she's given herself permission to inform others of that fact. Those close to her know she will not tolerate teasing.

She reinforced the boundary. We rarely set boundaries and then ignore them. Christie has not only informed me about this one, but when it's been violated, she's firmly reminded me of the importance of this boundary to her. She's reinforced it.

She makes self-care an ongoing priority. Boundaries must be managed on an ongoing basis. Christie cares about herself and believes she has the right to guard against any tendency of others to tease her. Can she stop anyone from teasing her? Of course not. But she can remove herself from their presence, and this is a powerful tool.

So while we don't have lines on the roads of our minds, we can teach people how to treat us, thereby creating markers for them to remember as they interact and travel with us. These instructions for others about how we expect to be treated become the markers on the road they can choose to attend to if they want to be in relationship with us, including in marriage.

Reinforced Boundaries

We can't set boundaries and then forget about them. If only it were that simple. Wouldn't it be nice if we could announce how we want to be treated only once and then have it set in stone? What if others heard us, attended to our concerns, and automatically stayed in their own lane? But life isn't that simple.

Sometimes boundaries have to be reinforced, strengthened, and even heightened to have their desired impact. Remember, however, we teach others how to treat us. If we won't manage our boundaries, reinforcing them with escalating consequences for violations, people won't honor them. If we're not crystal clear with consequences, we can't expect other people to honor them.

Said another way, if we're not serious about our values and boundaries, knowing what our business is and ensuring we're clear with others about these values, we shouldn't expect others to know and honor them.

Another boundaries situation occurred in my marriage a few years ago. When driving, I had the bad habits of coming to an incomplete stop and failing to use my turn signals. This had both annoyed and frightened Christie over the years, but I dismissed her complaints as "excessive sensitivity," and thus the problem persisted.

Notice several critical points here:

1. *Christie merely complained.* A boundary without consequences is not a boundary; it's a hope, wish, or complaint. Complaining has little power to change behavior.

2. *I dismissed her feelings.* I made the problem about Christie, not about my behavior. I didn't want to be bothered by her needs, which impacted how I continued to drive.

3. *I lacked empathy for Christie's feelings.* Because I blamed Christie for being "too sensitive," I didn't feel a need to change. I was in denial, and I didn't take ownership of the problem.

4. *So the problem persisted.* Problems persist without clear boundaries with clear consequences.

This problem persisted, as problems tend to do, until something radically shifted. I remember where and when this conversation took place.

"David," Christie said. We had come to a stop sign. "I've decided unless you come to complete stops and use your turn signals, I'm not riding with you. I don't feel safe. We can still go places together, but we'll drive separately."

Her message was that clear and concise, and it had consequences. By the power of her boundary and willingness to enforce it, I was forced to review my behavior. Her action was, in effect, *an invitation for change*, which is exactly what boundaries are—an invitation for someone to respond favorably, keeping a relationship intact and healthy.

I wish I could tell you I immediately responded favorably, but I didn't. Yet her message was clear. Whose business was it to manage her fear? Hers. Did she have the power to choose to ride with me or not? Absolutely. Was her boundary clear? Yes.

After a bit of consternation, though, I reflected on her boundary and decided I wanted her to ride with me. More important, I wanted to be a man who both cared about his wife's feelings and drove safely. I decided to change.

Kudos to Christie for teaching people how to treat her. Kudos to me for allowing her feelings to impact me and to realign my values to be the kind of man I really want to be.

Invitation to Change

Christie's actions that day led to an awakening in me. Again, should I have heard her message before? Of course. But beyond complaints, boundaries must be set, and they often have to be repeated more clearly, with consequences forcing the offending person to make a decision— to respond favorably or not.

The choice is *always* theirs. We can't *make* anyone do anything. We can only send a clear message that teaches others how we expect to be treated. Then when we've been clear, concise, and consistent, they're faced with the invitation to change.

Assumptions and Blind Spots

Unfortunately, most people don't have clear, definitive boundaries with consequences for those who trespass. They have preferences, to be sure. They feel annoyed when others trespass in their emotional space.

They have a sense of what is in their lane and what is not in their lane. But they wrongly assume that others will be sensitive and respectful of their boundaries.

Some people are even indignant about others trespassing, assuming everyone should just know to stay out of their business. This is faulty thinking. Others should not be expected to automatically know their values and protect them. Again, that is our business and responsibility to communicate.

Step back and consider what boundaries you've set in your life—or should. Make a list of your values, what's most important to you. Is it critical to be treated with respect? What boundaries have you put in place to ensure that happens, especially in your marriage? Is it imperative to feel love? What boundaries have you set to enforce love being part of your life?

Again, as you reflect on boundaries you have set, consider if you've been crystal clear, concise, and consistent—with consequences. Remember Christie's actions with me and my driving. She offered a very clear choice. Either way, she would be protected, and that responsibility was and is hers to enforce.

Self-Awareness As It Relates to Others

An awareness of ourselves as it relates to others in the world is key to setting boundaries and respecting others' boundaries. We need a clear sense of how our actions impact others.

This is a refined skill and one worth working on. Think about it. Imagine having no awareness of how you impact those around you. We all know people like that. They're like the proverbial bull in a china shop, banging into people at will. Unaware of their actions and presence, these people have no source of feedback. They wrongly presume any problem is someone else's responsibility. They have no need to change since they believe any problem has little to do with them. Of course, they're wrong. They're no fun to be around, and they frustrate everyone in their vicinity.

Quite amazingly, they have little awareness of any of this, even in a marriage.

Now imagine being a person who is keenly aware of your presence with others. You move through the world with confidence, self-assured but aware of how you impact other people. With a constant source of feedback, you can adjust your actions according to the need of the moment. You can avoid ongoing boundary problems in your marriage.

We can become better traveling companions, but we must be aware of ourselves. We must be watchful and speak up when someone—even our mate—strays into our lane.

When Awareness of Ourselves Is on the Blink

I'm amazed that most people have never cultivated this awareness. They've failed to refine their ability to monitor their actions, grown insensitive to their mate, or chosen to move through the world in whatever way they want.

You know the type. They're likely to say things like this:

"It's not my problem."

"People will think what they're going to think."

"I couldn't care less."

"People are too sensitive."

"I don't really care what people think."

Can you imagine moving through the world without really caring what people think? Could you really move through the world not caring if people were concerned about your behavior? What kind of traveling companion would that make for the person you married?

I hope this depiction doesn't fit you, but I don't think you would be reading this if you were that insensitive. You likely care about what people think and want feedback about your behavior. This gives you the opportunity to grow and expand your awareness. To maintain sensitivity, however, takes cultivating your awareness of self as it relates to others.

Signs You Need Boundaries

Most of us need ongoing work on boundaries. This isn't something you can learn, do, and then relax.

Perhaps you've grown insensitive to other's boundaries. You may have lost a sense of others and their preferences, or you're in relationship with someone with little awareness of how they move through the world. You may have struggled with so much conflict that now you're insensitive to your mate and their boundaries.

Don't worry. If you're experiencing any of these scenarios, you're in good company. We'll talk about how to handle it if you're in a relationship with a boundary-buster. We all can learn more about staying in our own lane and, in so doing, making our relationships healthier.

Kimberly Montgomery, in her article "Signs That You May Need to Set Healthier Boundaries," offers this counsel: "People who lack healthy boundaries are often emotionally needy (therapy speak: codependent). They have a poor sense of self and are desperate for love and validation from others. They 'give themselves up' in exchange for love and attention."[13]

Here are six signs you may need firmer, clearer boundaries. Some of them are adapted from Montgomery's article.

1. You feel angry and taken advantage of.

2. You wish others were sensitive to your feelings and needs.

3. You "rescue" people.

4. You become enmeshed in other's problems, wishing you hadn't.

5. Your relationships are chaotic.

6. You push away from people because of their insensitivity.

If you see yourself in any of these signs—especially when it comes to your marriage—you need more work in this area of your life. While you may believe the problem lies with others, more often it probably arises because your boundaries lack clarity and enforcement.

Boundary-busters continue their poor behavior, driving outside their lane, because someone like you tolerates it.

I have good news, however. We can become more knowledgeable about boundary-busters, and we can manage our lives more effectively. But first we must do some inner work—learning about what is important to us and where and how to establish lanes for our life.

The answer, then, is not to tell others to be different but for us to be different. We must attend to the neediness within us that leads us to rescue others. We must provide validation to ourselves rather than seek it from others. The exchange of attention for our time and energy isn't worth the trade.

Boundary-Busters

As I've said, no one can crash our boundaries without our consent. I know this is a hard truth, but it's also empowering.

A "boundary-buster" is someone who strays from their lane into ours. And not only do they stray from their lane but they drive all over the proverbial road.

Not all boundary-busters are, however, created equal; they tend to function on a spectrum. At one end are those who are more benign. They violate your boundaries by taking up too much of your time or emotional energy without intending to do so. These people are simply unaware of their actions, and usually a soft, clear message will help them tune in to your boundaries. "I'm really busy this afternoon, so I can't talk right now," you might say. "But tomorrow I'll have more time, and I'll be happy to talk then."

Assuming the other person has some self-awareness, such instruction will be met with a courteous response. Many people like clear boundaries. They want to know where they stand with you and what boundaries you need to be in good emotional health.

Near the other end of the spectrum of boundary-busters are those who simply don't get it and don't seem to want to get it, and they seem intent on staying that way. They want to drive around as if the entire road is theirs. They dislike boundaries and may get upset when you try

to set them. "No" doesn't mean no; it signals an opportunity to manipulate and push even more.

At the extreme end of the spectrum are those who violently push
their weight around. They shout, get angry, and act out in the face
of boundaries. They want control, and they'll do anything to get it.
These people, of course, are dangerous, and they harm everyone in
their path.

Our task, though—and it *is* ours—is the same with all people:
to set, establish, and maintain healthy boundaries. We must inform
them about what is important to us, inviting them into our lives if,
and only if, they honor and respect who we are and what is important to us. We must not rant and rave about their behavior, taking on
the role of victim. While this may feel good for a moment, it won't
get us anywhere. Only focusing on ourselves and how we're feeling
changes anything.

Growing Healthy Relationships

Not only do we have the power to stay in our own lane but we
also have the power to associate only with those who stay in theirs,
to grow and cultivate healthy relationships. This is a dynamic process, ever changing. Teaching people how to treat us is an ongoing
process, not a once-and-for-all situation. We must continually share
with others how we'd like to be treated, evaluating how they respond
in the process.

While we can't completely control who's around us—such as in the
workplace—we can choose who we want as friends. We can befriend
people with healthy boundaries. We can seek out those who stay in
their own lane and show respect for our lane and preferences.

I've found it critical to associate with people who work on staying
in their lane. Those who are reckless regarding boundaries tend to be
chaos-creators. If someone isn't sensitive to and respectful of my feelings, as well as to the needs I have to be healthy, I don't need them in
my life.

What about friendships where the person causes you more

headaches than positivity? Reconsider those where you feel consistently taken advantage of or when you're with people who seem insensitive to your requests for healthy boundaries. Trying to hang on to those friendships tends not to work. We don't help anyone by holding on to a friendship that needs to end.

Refocusing

Your task when it comes to boundaries, then, is to refocus. Step back, size up where you are, and determine how *you* can stay in your lane while asking others to stay in theirs. Remember, you can't make others do anything. All you can do is invite them to change as you focus on changing your own behavior.

Before you set out to "stay in your lane," ensure you've looked within and taken care of any need or desire to control others or manage their behavior. This is wasted energy. Remember, their life is their life, and they get to do with it what they want. If you're managing someone else's life, you're doing them no good and you're not managing your own life. You're not staying in your lane.

Furthermore, others will resent you. They know you're trying to change them. They know you're trying to manipulate their behavior, and they will dislike it. They will push away from you, leaving you with even less influence on them.

When we focus on ourselves, though, we're much more likely to work on ourselves and stay in our own lane. Focusing on ourselves, while also remaining sensitive to others, keeps us out of someone else's business. Appreciating others and their values is an incredible way to love and honor them, thereby doing our part to create healthy relationships.

The next time you're troubled, ask yourself if you're in your own lane or if you're trying to get someone else to change. Again, this doesn't mean we can't ask others to change—we just can't insist on it. We can only invite others to change, sharing our feelings and hoping they'll care and allow our feelings to impact them. If they really care about us, they will be impacted.

Maintaining Emotional Balance

Staying in our lane helps us maintain emotional balance, and maintaining emotional balance helps us stay in our lane.

Think about this. It goes both ways. When we practice emotional balance, our thought life is controlled. We think more clearly. We manage our emotions and thus make better decisions.

It works the other way as well. As we make better decisions, thinking through our choices, our emotional life follows suit; we're happier and more content.

Maintaining emotional balance isn't just a good thing to do. We're told in Scripture to "be quick to listen, slow to speak and slow to anger" (James 1:19). This is a powerful directive, taking emotional awareness and self-control, another fruit of the Spirit. When I'm quick to hear, I'm appreciating others. When I'm slow to speak, I don't take myself so seriously. I see others for who they are, recognizing they're in their own world, not necessarily in mine.

All this was put to the test for Christie and me as we flew back from Cape Cod. We had traveled all day, and we were looking forward to landing in Seattle. However, Seattle was experiencing a freak thunderstorm, and our flight was rerouted to Spokane, 300 miles east of Seattle.

We were tired, testy, and irritable, as were most of the other 150 passengers. Add to this challenging situation ticketing agents who were less than helpful. (They were likely tired and irritable too.) I was aware of wanting to lash out at one impatient agent. But I was also aware that getting angry with her would serve no purpose and only create more unrest in an already trying situation.

Christie and I shared a few frustrations with this agent, but for the most part we held back our critical thoughts. We reminded each other we were tired and might say things we would later regret. We tried to maintain awareness of what was our business and what was not, as well as what was in our lane and what was not. These decisions are all the more difficult when feeling emotionally unbalanced.

What are some strategies we can practice when feeling tired and unsteady emotionally?

Stop or at least slow down. We feel much faster than we can think, so it's important to slow down.

Think. What are we feeling and why are we feeling it? What exactly are these emotions and what do they say about me?

Consider how you want to act. Remind yourself that no one can make you act a certain way. You have control over how you view a situation and how you behave. Don't give others the power to challenge you to act in ways you'll regret.

Choose the better way. Behave the way you ideally want to be. Act right, and soon your thoughts and emotions will follow.

Defensive Driving

Notice that it's not enough to stay in your lane; you must also maintain some space between the lanes. Imagine being in a car, staying in your lane but with only inches to spare between you and the car in the next lane. Would you still feel safe?

It's always good to be aware of other drivers when traveling. This is called defensive driving, and we're taught to leave enough room between us and other cars. To anticipate danger. To see challenging situations before we're caught up in them.

This is a powerful principle as it applies to relationships—especially to the marriage relationship. By using good judgment, we can anticipate a problematic situation. We can anticipate the impact of our words. We can seek to understand others, measuring our response and reaction to their temperament and needs. And by using good judgment, we can sense when our traveling companion needs a bit of extra space or grace.

I remember such a situation several years ago. I had done what I told myself I would never again do—fly home on a Sunday evening. I was hungry and tired, and when I walked through the door of my house, I was ready to pick a fight. Why? Because I was hungry and tired—no other reason.

As I started to do so with my wife over something innocuous but important to me because of my distorted, tired thinking, Christie had the mindfulness to drive defensively.

"David," she said softly but firmly, "you're tired, and I think this would be a better conversation for the morning—if it's still important to you then."

"But I want to talk about it now."

"No. I'll talk about it with you in the morning when we're both rested—if it's still important to you then."

I reluctantly conceded, and we went to bed.

It was not important in the morning.

Moral of the story? Active listening, emotional balance, and defensive driving. Leave things alone unless you're really in a good space to talk about them *and* they're in your lane.

And So, What About Love?

Stepping outside the topic of marriage for a moment, let's again consider all our relationships when it comes to boundaries.

Love and friendship drew us to the people in our lives, but just because we care about them doesn't mean they're healthy for us. Sometimes we must step back and reevaluate. *Am I being clear about my needs with the people in my life? Am I choosing to associate with those who respect my boundaries? Do I need to share my concerns with someone so we both can see if the relationship can change for the better?*

Take time to evaluate your boundaries and those with whom you've chosen to share your life. Do they honor and respect the boundaries of others? We learned in this chapter that boundary-setting is a dynamic, ongoing process; it never stops. We teach people how to treat us. If we're feeling mistreated on a consistent basis, we're participating in a destructive process, and we must make changes.

So do it. Set some positive goals, change your interactions—especially with your spouse—and see what happens.

Now let's explore the power and importance of knowing and healing our feelings on the marriage journey.

9

WATCHING YOUR WARNING LIGHTS

Preventative Maintenance in Marriage

*Things never go wrong at
the moment you expect them to.*
C.K. KELLY MARTIN

don't often think about the warning lights on the dashboard in my car. They're easy for me to ignore, and I figure if something really bad is about to happen, I'll hear a ding or a buzz or see the light flashing soon enough to take action.

This is not always the case, though. Sometimes a flashing light indicates it's too late for me to take effective action. The manufacturer of the car installed warning lights for a reason—the protection of the car and ultimately for the sake of my well-being.

I've lived my life paying too little attention to relational warning lights, assuming nothing would go wrong. Then when it did—and of course it did—I was taken by surprise. Intellectually, I've known the best way to deal with problems is preventing them in the first place (preventative maintenance), but I've pretended problems wouldn't arise because I didn't want to think about them.

This is "magical thinking." I have been foolish, thinking if I didn't see and experience a problem, then it didn't exist.

This is clearly not a good way to live life. I miss out on cues, signals, and alarms that could ward off potential problems. This thinking is also called DENIAL—[I] Don't Even Notice I Am Lying [to myself]. As I did in an earlier chapter, I refer to this acronym often because it's so informative. Denial is wishful thinking—thinking everything will work out naturally, spontaneously. Again, this is foolish, and it's a tendency I'm working on.

In this chapter we'll learn about the warning lights, signs, and information systems known as emotions—*energy in motion*—that send us signals many times a day, informing us we feel good or we feel bad. These emotions offer invaluable information to navigate through life with others, including our marriage partner. Knowing what we feel and sensing what others around us feel offers us critical information on how to best proceed.

Living in a Fog

Living in denial, avoiding warning lights (emotions), unaware of what is happening inside you and between you and within your mate, is a sure path to problems. Ignoring your warning lights is like living in a fog.

Remember, you've chosen to move through life with a traveling companion, so recognizing your inner signals, combined with your mate's signals, is critical. This partnership demands attention and timely interaction.

Imagine for a moment driving without warning lights. Imagine driving without any instrumentation to tell you your speed or gas consumption. Suddenly, these lights become even more important. And emotions are our reference points in life, giving vital information.

Each of us experiences emotions multiple times a day. Your significant relationships, the people in your life you've chosen to journey with, all have their own daily signals (emotions). Those signals, in combination with yours, bring challenges and the need to pay close attention to everything happening both within you and between you.

Living relational life effectively must incorporate understanding your emotions. Emotions—joy, sadness, fear, anger, and many others—inform us how we're getting along with those around us moment by moment. They inform us what might need adjusting, a change in direction or course for our life.

Remember, our internal maps and compasses must be reviewed periodically, and without updated guidance and with warning lights disconnected, we tend to meander—we're in a fog. We set course one time and keep going, regardless of how our circumstances may have changed. We fail to pick up on cues, inspirations, and changing conditions important for us to attend to, and subsequently, we become lost.

What happens if we're lost? What if our mate is sending signals critical to the welfare of our relationship but we disregard them? We vowed to stay tuned in to our mate and others in our care. They have feelings, preferences, and changing inclinations. What if we settled into living in a state of lazy unhappiness that could have been avoided?

Worse, what if our traveling companion is just as lost? Who is leading the journey?

Remember what I've said about the power of listening effectively, tuning in to your mate. Tuning in means listening to their feelings. Recall this person has their own preferences, inclinations, and feelings. They have warning lights to which they may or may not be attending.

Living life unaware, ignoring feelings hidden beneath the surface on your part and on theirs, leads to real problems. Eruptions occur when you least expect them, when feelings mount, and when conflict recurs though you thought everything was fine.

Feelings as Warnings

Again, our emotions are warning lights, powerful sources of information. And again, our emotions can be viewed as energy in motion. I like this definition because it suggests a feeling such as joy, sorrow, or anger moves us as well as informs us. These emotions create meaning in our life.

Imagine walking in the door of your home after a long day at work.

You're tired and ready to relax. You plop down on the couch, vaguely noticing your mate is moody. Something seems to be upsetting them. The emotion in the room is heavy, and you have a decision to make. Will you attend to your mate and their emotion? Or will you continue relaxing on the couch?

Your experience has suddenly changed. Your warning lights are working—you notice a tightening in your chest, perhaps feeling apprehension. You begin asking yourself questions to make sense of the situation. Has your mate experienced a bad day? Is something upsetting them? Are they upset with you?

You decide to ask, "Is everything okay?"

You paid attention to the warning lights signaling something seemed to be amiss. Your emotion moved you to ask a question, to make a connection. In all likelihood you can now have a meaningful conversation. You can be a listening ear to what is bothering your mate or resolve any issue that might have occurred between you.

Now imagine living disconnected—from both your feelings and those of your mate. What happens if you ignore your spouse's signals? What if they even make a more obvious gesture indicating they're in distress? If you ignore those signals and you're not moved to action, further problems can arise, making a small problem a larger one, probably amplifying existing emotions.

Your mate's warning lights, and yours, are flashing.

Can you see how watching and attending to emotions are like watching and attending to warning lights in your car? You can ignore them or disregard them, or you pay attention to them and allow them to help you understand what's happening in your relationship.

His Feelings/Her Feelings

A lot is often going on in our relationships. At any given time we likely face feelings of our own, involving our own matters; feelings of our mate, involving their own matters; and feelings between the two of us, involving matters pertaining to us both.

Whew!

Am I saying we must attend to all these signals all the time? Yes, if we want to ensure our relationship is functioning in the most efficient and effective way possible, we need to attend to ourselves, to our mates, and to the connection between us.

Again, whew!

If you're thinking *This is hard work*, you're right. We have no room in our relationships for emotional laziness. We have no time to sit back and assume this car (relationship) will run on autopilot. Coasting doesn't apply. Healthy relationships function on attentiveness and continual care.

But what about staying in our own lane? Doesn't that mean our mates take care of themselves and we take care of us? Yes and no. Our mates are responsible for the aspects of their life that belong to them. However some aspects of their well-being require protection on our part. Care, compassion, concern, and comfort are all aspects of their well-being that are partly our responsibility and vice versa. This is what I refer to as positive codependence, which we'll talk about more in a moment.

In a smooth-running relationship, emotional laziness has no place. Traveling together means attending to a combination of feelings—yours, your mate's, and the feelings between the two of you.

Creating a Safe Place for Feelings

If you're an external processor like me, you need safe places to talk out your feelings—to really tune in to your inner warning lights. You don't know what you think or feel until you've spoken out loud.

If you're an internal processor, preferring to work out issues in your head, expressing your emotions are ways of connecting with another person. Still, for that connection to happen, we must feel safe.

Safety and trust are huge issues for most couples. When pressed, many people say they do *not* feel safe sharing their most vulnerable feelings with their spouse. They're not convinced they care about their deepest feelings or concerns.

This, of course, creates barriers to intimacy. In marriage, intimacy—"into me see"—occurs when we feel safe sharing our innermost thoughts and feelings and our mate feels the same. Feeling safe and willing to be vulnerable, we share fully with each other, feeling close and connected.

Tamara Thompson, in her article "Talk to Me! 6 Ways to Create Emotional Safety in Your Relationship," considers steps we and our mate need to take. She also shares what damage is done when we don't take them.

1. *Listen Non-defensively:* Listen empathically to your mate and validate their concerns. Damage is done when you tell your mate not to feel the way they do, dismiss their feelings, or talk over them.

2. *Let Go of Toxic Thoughts About Your Partner:* Let go of labels you've used to describe your mate, such as stubborn, lazy, or weak. Open yourself to seeing your spouse in a new light. Damage is done when you assume they will never change or when you see them only as they were in the past.

3. *Realize That Body Language and Touch Matter:* Body language matters a great deal in creating safe, emotional space. Turn toward your mate, give them eye contact, sit close, and touch their hands. Give them your undivided attention. Damage is done when you sit distantly and appear distracted.

4. *Emphasize and Reinforce Commitment:* Express commitment to your mate, staying emotionally connected. Routinely share your love and care for them. Damage is done when you reference the possibility of divorce, moving out, or leaving the relationship, leading your mate to feeling insecure and unsafe, triggering old wounds.

5. *Thank Them:* It's important to thank your mate for sharing their emotions. Regardless of how you feel, thank your spouse for trusting you enough to share their vulnerability with you. Say you appreciate learning more about them.

Damage is done when you don't acknowledge your mate's vulnerability and their courage to share.

6. *Be Consistent:* Consistency builds trust because we know what to expect. Your mate needs to learn you'll be there for them, that you'll do what you say you will do. Damage is done when you don't keep your promises, treating them lovingly one day and withdrawing another. Damage is done when commitments aren't kept.[14]

You and your mate have embarked on a momentous journey together, and the trip requires deep trust. Creating emotional safety provides an environment where you both share what's happening within you and between you. Like warning lights in a car, these feelings will *move you* to understanding the next action to take.

Share Feelings, Not Judgments

Even if you've created emotional safety, sharing emotions isn't easy. We often believe we're being vulnerable, sharing feelings, when in fact we're sharing opinions and thoughts. It's a common mistake, having huge ramifications for our relationships.

In his book *Nonviolent Communication*, Dr. Marshall Rosenberg explains this problem: "A common confusion, generated by the English language, is our of the word *feel* without actually expressing a feeling. For example, in the sentence, 'I feel I didn't get a fair deal,' the words *I feel* could be more accurately replaced with *I think*."[15]

He goes on to share some words that only complicate this common problem:

"I feel *that* you should know better."

"I feel *like* a failure."

"I feel *as if* I'm living with a wall."[16]

The words *that, like,* and *as if* express opinions and judgments, often

creating tension between you and your mate. Believing you're sharing feelings when, in fact, you're sharing judgments is likely to lead to
defensiveness in your mate.

This is not hard to understand when you think about it. Sharing
feelings is about *you*, while sharing judgments is about *them*. Sharing
feelings is about what's happening within *you*, offering information.
Sharing judgments is about *the other person* and often involves something pointed and potentially hurtful.

I've found that many marriage partners make these mistakes, and
I noticed them in the relationship of a couple I worked with recently.

Jeff and Maggie

Jeff and Maggie, married for only three years, came for a couple's
counseling session. They indicated meeting with me was their last
attempt to save their marriage.

"Tell me about your relationship," I said.

"We really love each other," Maggie said, smiling and touching her
husband's leg affectionately. Jeff reached back, touching her hand. "But
our relationship is like a bad roller coaster ride. We never know when
we'll have an eruption, and when it does, watch out."

"What does that mean?" I asked. "What happens when things
erupt?"

Jeff and Maggie looked at each other, then Jeff spoke.

"We've been known to stay up arguing for hours," he said. "She
won't stop. She follows me around."

I looked to Maggie for her input.

"I just want him to talk to me. I don't want to fight. I don't like fighting. I want to share my feelings."

"But you don't tell me your feelings," Jeff said in protest. "You argue
with me."

"I feel pushed away by you. I feel like you don't listen to me when
I'm upset. When we have issues we need to resolve, all you care about
is getting sleep."

I listened, reflecting on what Maggie was likely feeling, but more importantly on *how* she was communicating her needs. While she was no doubt in a lot of distress, she was making many of the errors Rosenberg talks about, likely only exacerbating their communication problems.

Let's review Maggie's message to Jeff to see what part of their problem might be.

1. Maggie shares she feels *pushed away* by Jeff. Rather than sharing a feeling, she shares a judgment *against* him. She says she's pushed away by him rather than sharing she feels *alone and frightened*.

2. Maggie shares she feels *like Jeff doesn't listen*. Again, although she's attacking him, pushing him away, she actually feels *unheard and alone*.

3. Finally, Maggie accuses Jeff of *caring only about getting sleep*. While he certainly may care about sleep, only he knows his concerns and values.

Let's assume both Jeff and Maggie communicate in this manner. Imagine they believe they're sharing feelings when they're actually sharing accusations, opinions, and judgments. Can you see how this pattern leads to escalations in communication? Can you further see how they miss speaking to each other in vulnerable, connecting ways?

What if instead of speaking in vague, accusatory language, Maggie shared the following: "Jeff, I've been feeling lonely. I really want to connect with you and spend some time talking. How about if we go out to dinner together?"

Can you imagine how much safer Jeff and Maggie would feel in discussing their issues if she did?

Learning a Feelings Vocabulary

Jeff and Maggie are like many of us—ignoring warning lights until they're flashing, indicating real trouble. When they finally do attend to the warning lights, emotions have reached a higher pitch, making it more likely both of them will say things in ways that add to their problems.

What we say and how we say it are critical aspects of communication. In Jeff and Maggie's efforts to share feelings, they use language that is provocative, accusatory, blaming, and shaming, creating even more disconnection and inhibiting effective problem-solving.

While Maggie is now tuning in to her warning lights, she's still not able to articulate her feelings well. She actually responds to Jeff in a way that adds more alarm and damage to the situation.

What needs to change? How might she share her feelings in a way she can connect to Jeff and increase her chance of being heard?

We must create a vocabulary for our feelings, understanding *a feeling is a feeling*. It's not as easy as we often think. Maggie may feel *alone, sad, hurt, frightened*. She doesn't *feel like, that*, or *as if*. We feel *feelings* and *think* opinions and judgments—and opinions and judgments, if shared at all, must be shared ever so cautiously. They often have a bite to them, and we must recognize that.

While changing how you say things may seem overly difficult, it *is* important. If you do, you'll notice a difference in your relationship. Sharing vulnerable feelings connects; accusations create disconnection. Vulnerable feelings draw our mates to us; accusations push them away.

We must all learn these truths and put them into practice in our relationships. When working with couples, I use a recipe many have found helpful, so I think it's worth learning, practicing, and sharing with your mate. Using Maggie as an example, she could share the following:

- *Say what you feel.* "I feel lonely."

- *Say what you'd like to feel.* "I'd like to feel connected and loved."

- *Share a specific, positive request.* "I'd like us to set aside a time to be together every evening."

Notice Maggie, if using these tools, would be sharing what she feels and what she wants to feel and then connecting both of those to a specific request Jeff is likely to agree to. This becomes a win-win situation.

Limiting yourself to these three points will help you be heard while creating a safe place for your mate. This recipe is free from any accusations or judgments. Most of us are tempted to share far more, explaining our point and pushing for a certain outcome, thus increasing tension. This will not help. No one wants to feel pushed. Less is more. Simpler is better. Give your mate the best opportunity to respond to your need.

Feelings and Vulnerability

Expressing our needs, clearly and simply, increases the likelihood of having them met. Again, free from accusations and speaking vulnerably, you want to stay connected to your mate. You want to be heard, as do they. *Vulnerability is the only way to have our feelings—our warning lights—attended to.*

Vulnerability draws others to us. This is a universal truth. We're drawn to people willing to share their weakness, their humanity. We tend to identify with people willing to show their fragility, feeling compassion for them.

Opinions, accusations, and judgments are more detached, less vulnerable forms of communication. Judgments are often delivered with an air of self-righteousness, putting others on edge. Even unintended, judgments don't draw your mate to you but rather push them away. Why is that?

Think about it this way. Consider again how Maggie shared her feelings with Jeff: "I feel pushed away by you. I feel like you don't listen to me." These are actually thoughts about how she feels, *not* her vulnerable feelings. She shared what she hoped would draw him to her, but what she was really doing was attacking him—a mistake many make. He then reacted, feeling threatened. Guarding against feeling vulnerable, he defended himself, making him unavailable to really hear her.

Jeff's reaction was predictable. He likely felt unsafe and reacted accordingly, creating an even greater gap between them. Regardless of Maggie's approach, however, Jeff is still responsible for his response. We never have to react. We can listen for the feeling beneath the accusation, to what our mate is trying to say, though we may have to work through our own feelings of threat to really hear them.

Maggie and Jeff's dilemma brings the same challenge we all face—trying to share our feelings in a way that connects us to our mate rather than pushes them away. We all want to be heard, but we must take responsibility for how we share. We are all responsible for speaking vulnerably, the way we truly connect with each other.

Connecting/Disconnecting Emotions

Maggie and Jeff's story offers us an insight into emotions that connect and emotions that disconnect. Only after each person takes responsibility for their words, sending the message they wish to send, will they choose more frequently to connect.

Solomon wisely said, "The tongue has the power of life and death" (Proverbs 18:21). We must each take responsibility for how we talk to our mate. Understanding what connects and disconnects gives us immense influence over others.

It's important we see Maggie is not out of line with her concerns. She's simply misguided. She *feels* alone and hurt and wants to be heard. She wants to feel cared for and valued. Her warning lights are working. But if she doesn't take time to consider what to do with those warning lights, how to best convey what she wants to convey, she may create more trouble for herself.

While our emotions are healthy and God-given, we must harness them and decipher what they mean to us. We must then determine how best to say what we really want to say. We must be vigilant to guard against impulsive reaction, and this is critical to healthy relating.

Many of us feel our warning lights/emotions and then react. We yell, speak harshly, or blurt out opinions without really thinking. Remember, we feel much faster than we think. If Maggie is overwhelmed by her anger and frustration, she has less ability to think clearly. She is less efficient in her decision-making, unable to communicate as clearly as she might. Speaking in accusatory, blaming, and shaming language, she plays a major role in her disconnection with Jeff.

If Maggie takes time to slow down and think, she'll be able to use more vulnerable, connecting emotions—sadness, hurt, loneliness—and function much more effectively. This affords her the possibility of staying clear and centered, emotionally balanced, leading to more flexibility in her thinking. Feeling more balanced, she can then choose her words more carefully.

We would all do well to remember our primary goal for communicating—*to connect*. Anything we do that opposes or interrupts that goal won't be useful to us.

Again, we feel much more quickly than we think. Our warning lights flash, signaling emotions being triggered. If we don't slow down, we're likely to react *before* thinking everything through. Feeling before thinking, leading to feeling overwhelmed, often leads to greater problems.

Flooding

What do we do when our feelings, those warning lights that signal us, overwhelm us? How do we guard against being defensive when feeling flooded?

We're able to process only a certain amount of information at one time, and so we must have the ability to manage our emotions when we feel overwhelmed.

The emotion of anger often adds to feelings of being overwhelmed. While anger is a legitimate feeling, it often gets us into trouble. Feeling angry when emotionally upset often makes it hard to think clearly. When flooded by feelings of anger, we focus on a perceived slight. We feel righteously indignant. We want a wrong rectified.

Nothing is necessarily wrong with these thoughts or feelings, but we must be aware of the inclination to say things we'll regret later, especially when we're angry. We're often reckless. Our bodies are physiologically responding in a fight-or-flight mode, neither of which is likely to help us think clearly and make wise choices. Our heart rhythms become erratic. Scientists know the heart and brain are connected.

With smoother heart rhythms, we're more likely to make better decisions.

So what should we do when the warning lights come on? It's always wise to slow down, breathe deeply and evenly, and consider what actions you want to take. Think. Think ahead. What is your goal and the best way of reaching that goal? The warning lights—your emotions—are signals giving you information. It's up to you to use the information wisely.

Bad Moods

When feelings are particularly intense, it's tempting to slip into a bad mood. And who hasn't slipped into one? I certainly have.

Several weeks ago the check engine light came on in my car again—a literal warning light. As I told you earlier, it had come on before, indicating the need for a costly repair. Seeing the light now, a few months later, I panicked.

My feelings didn't stop there, however. I felt increasingly unsettled, anxious, and frightened. I worried that my car would need another costly repair. I imagined the worst, and I slipped into a bad mood.

Unfortunately, extreme thinking often leads to more extreme thinking. Warning lights—emotions—are misread and misleading. In my situation my panic led to more discouragement, and I was moody about the situation until I had my mechanic diagnose the problem. As it turned out, no repair was needed.

Elijah's Bad Mood

Elijah of the Bible slipped into a bad mood I'll call temporary insanity.

While he had reason to be upset, Elijah did what many of us do—he misread his warning lights and reacted emotionally. Then he slipped into a really bad mood. Let's consider what we might learn from his situation.

While I like Elijah, he didn't manage his feelings well. Here's a guy who at one time was standing atop Mount Carmel in victory, and now, a short time later, he's cowering in a cave wishing to die.

Wow. What happened?

As the story goes, Elijah had just returned from a showdown with the false prophets of Baal. He prayed down fire from heaven, and as a result, a nation turned back to God. This was pretty powerful stuff.

Then even more positive things happened. He asked God to restore rain for the first time in over three years. Again, powerful stuff. You would think this would increase Elijah's confidence and help insure him from moodiness in the future, but this was not the case.

Elijah continued to experience blessings from God, and he did well while things were going his way. He was in great spirits. But good times are not always enough insulation against a bad mood. Sometimes warning lights are working but misread.

The situation worsens for Elijah. He receives a death threat from Jezebel, King Ahab's evil queen. Her message to him? "By this time tomorrow, you're a dead man" (1 Kings 19:2, paraphrase mine). This powerful prophet of God, who had confronted a wicked king, led a nation to repentance, and faced down false prophets, felt overwhelmed by the threat of one woman. So Elijah fled from Jezreel to Beersheba, over one hundred miles away, collapsing in the wilderness under a juniper tree. And this is where temporary insanity comes in, because there he asked God to take his life.

What is happening here? Why did Elijah feel happy one day and depressed the next? Because he was in a bad mood, overwhelmed by emotion, misreading warning lights. He felt understandably discouraged, emotionally and physically drained, needing rest, food, and a reprieve from stress we can all relate to.

Elijah was human, and in that state, he wasn't thinking clearly. No one does when they're exhausted. He was discouraged and needed support and encouragement.

Listen Well to Emotions

Here's another takeaway from Elijah's life as well as from Maggie's and mine: *We must listen well to our emotions.* Said another way, we must continue to feel yet learn from our emotions.

Shutting off emotions is a path many choose to escape pain. But they must be felt and allowed to inform us. When we close off one feeling, we close off all feelings. As much as we might want to escape feeling painful emotions, we just can't. All feelings are valuable to us. All feelings inform us. Even Elijah's feelings of weariness and discouragement were informative. My feelings of discouragement over my car were informative. Maggie's feelings of hurt and loneliness are informative. Not only are our hurts an integral part of our personality and functioning but our feelings help us know what we need and create a beautiful bridge to our mate.

If we are to heal our deepest hurts, we must feel them. We must ask ourselves a series of questions. *What emotion am I feeling? Why am I feeling this emotion? What does this emotion reveal about me? What do I need? What might I ask for to assist me in meeting my need?* All these questions help discover what might be needed to bring about healing.

Again, *you can't heal what you can't feel*. We must feel our feelings to create a healing opportunity.

Slow Down and Step Back

Feeling our feelings is a tougher challenge than you might expect. You may be thinking, *Of course I feel my feelings. I can't help but feel them.*

Not so fast. Remember, most of us certainly *feel* our feelings; we know the warning lights are flashing. But we don't correctly identify our feelings or take the time to fully understand them. We don't create a space to fully embrace our feelings. We're inclined to feel *something* and then react, but we don't take the time or the space to really understand our feelings.

What should we do instead?

We must slow down. This really is *the* answer for all of us. Take time to think, being mindful of what is happening in your marriage and what you want to happen. It takes time and space to really think things through. It takes time and space to reflect on how you want to handle the current situation.

We must step back from the situation. When we feel angry, our thoughts tend to narrow, we naturally think accusatorily, and our compassion for our mate fades. If we want to handle the situation most effectively, we must step back, take time out, and come back after emotions settle.

Helping Your Mate Heal

While emotions signal us to slow down and step back so we can analyze the situation and make our best decision, they also give us the opportunity to be mindful of our mate.

Jeff didn't have to become defensive. He could have stopped, settled his feelings, and considered what Maggie was trying to say to him. Yes, her reaction was disconnecting. She spoke in ways that would set most people on edge. Yet as we become more sophisticated and balanced in our own emotions, we become more capable of helping our mate to heal and respond more effectively. Jeff's reaction stopped Maggie from sharing more deeply.

While we don't know Jeff's feelings, we can presume he had feelings he would have liked to share. When our mate responds defensively, we can be sure something inside them is triggered. If we have created enough space within ourselves, if we are less reactive, we can hold space for our mate so they can share their emotions and needs. Both Maggie and Jeff must learn to create space for sharing feelings with each other going forward.

When interacting with our mate, we should have two questions in our minds at all times. They will both help us remain centered and guide us toward what our mate needs.

Let's consider them in some detail.

1. *What is my mate feeling?* Be curious, inviting the sharing of feelings. Pull for additional feelings. By focusing first on your spouse's need, you cultivate empathy, compassion, and most important, connection. Tuning in to their feelings helps you respond more effectively. You can do much to decrease the tension and work together to resolve the issue.

2. *What does my mate need?* Explore this in detail. Again, ask good questions. You have the opportunity to respond to the need of the moment. By focusing on first your spouse's feelings, then the underlying need, you connect with them in a powerful way. By identifying their need, you can do your part to meet that need.

Every place of difficulty is also filled with incredible opportunity. Whenever you interact with your mate, *you have the opportunity to consider what they're feeling* and *you have the opportunity to respond to the need of the moment.* By asking these questions, you can learn more about your mate and help bring healing.

Healing Together

We can heal together. And why not? We've chosen to travel with another person, and the travels are much more enjoyable if both of us are happy and healthy.

I'm reminded again that marriage is a partnership and, in a sense, we're only as healthy as we are together. When one of us flourishes, it's likely that both of us will flourish. But when one of us struggles, we both struggle.

So ask yourself if you're doing all you can to help your mate function optimally. Are you aware of their concerns, needs, and emotions? What do they need that you can provide to help them be as healthy as possible? Be aware of their general and specific concerns and respond effectively. If unaware, seek more information. Ask your mate to tell you more about their life and what they need to be healthier and happier.

And So, What About Love?

Throughout this book, we've been exploring what it takes to really make a relationship work after the initial "I do." We've learned again and again that the feeling of love was the glue that created the initial connection, but it takes so much more to continue that connection.

This chapter has been about paying attention to feelings—our warning lights—learning the difference between a feeling and a thought/opinion/judgment, and how to use our feelings more effectively to become aware of both our needs and those of our mate. We've learned you can't heal what you can't feel and that feeling our emotions is more difficult than we might at first think.

Feeling feelings is challenging, but it can be learned, and sharing more vulnerably is the best way possible to connect to your mate. Have fun practicing this powerful tool.

Moving forward again, let's explore how to keep our relationship tuned, understanding what it really takes to be aware of our issues, to own them, and to heal and change them.

10

KEEPING YOUR CAR TUNED

Taking Responsibility

*The beauty of my journey is that it's always
been pretty unpredictable, so stay tuned.*

ANDREJA PEJIC

I often consider going to *Consumer Reports* and researching the most reliable car on the road. Why? Because I hate taking my car to the mechanic. It takes far too much time and, in my opinion, costs far too much money. But my delight in driving a sports car overrides my fear of mechanics, so I settle for more temperamental cars, which usually need more frequent tune-ups and maintenance.

I cringe when I hear strange sounds from my car. This can only mean trouble, I surmise, and often I'm right. But my mechanic reminds me that if I care for regular maintenance, keeping my car tuned-up, I can avoid many of these problems.

Relationships have a considerable similarity to cars: We can do regular maintenance, keeping them tuned-up and avoiding costly repairs. For this to happen, however, we must stay very tuned in to our relationship, attend to warning signs, and take necessary action.

Perhaps much like me taking my car to the mechanic, it's common for couples to come to counseling saying they don't understand why their relationship has ups and downs, times of connection and times of significant disconnection.

"I don't know why it happens," Karen said to me during a counseling session. "We can be doing great, and then everything goes horribly, and we fight for days."

Karen and Daniel have been married for ten years and have two young children. Daniel works as a surveyor, and Karen works part-time as an accountant and cares for their children the days she's off.

"We have these long stretches of fighting," she continued, "followed by little moments of peace. That's just the way it is. I'd give anything if it was the other way around—long times of peace and love with only little blips of conflict. But it's not."

I've become accustomed to people sharing the way this woman shared with me. You can hear her feelings of defeat, and no wonder. She appears to feel little control over her life.

Notice that her language is passive, meaning she seems to believe her "long stretches of fighting, followed by little moments of peace" is the way it has to be. She speaks as if the conflict she has with her husband is inevitable, outside of her control.

This chapter focuses on a powerful but opposite truth: *If it's predictable, it's preventable.* Said another way, we have the responsibility and power to keep our relationship tuned-up. As we've learned in previous chapters, we can influence our mate in important ways. We have a great deal of influence over whether our relationship is working the way we want it to work.

It's Your Car; Keep It Tuned

In the last chapter, we discussed the importance of paying attention to warning lights—our emotions—for signals telling us the next right step to take. I want to build on this idea.

Imagine facing another kind of warning light: the flashing lights of a police car pulling you over for speeding.

The officer asks why you were speeding.

"I'm late for work," you say.

"Why?" the officer asks.

"Because I got up late."

"Why?" the officer asks again, continuing to probe.

At this point you're feeling a bit perplexed. You thought a simple response would satisfy. No, the officer wants to probe for deeper under-standing and responsibility.

"Because I stayed up too late, so I shut off my alarm," you say.

"Why did you stay up late if you knew you had to work in the morn-ing?" the officer says.

"I guess it was poor planning on my part."

The officer finally seems satisfied. "So you see," the officer contin-ues, "the problem didn't start with me pulling you over. It didn't start with you speeding. It didn't start with you turning off your alarm clock. It started yesterday with poor planning."

Our marriage journeys have similarities to the story of the speed-ing man. We've chosen to be in relationship with another person. That relationship takes ongoing care and feeding—tuning—much of which has to do with taking ownership of our part of the problem and our part in the solutions to the problems.

You Can't Change What You Don't Own

I want to share another story, this one about a man and a truck.

In a counseling session some time ago, I met Connie and Zack, a fortysomething couple who had been married for fifteen years. They were experiencing high conflict, and they hoped I could help them.

"We've seen many counselors," Connie began, "and none of them seem to help us really change. We fight as much as we ever have, and this is going to be our last effort. If you can't help us, we're ready to file for divorce."

I looked at Zack, who nodded his head in agreement.

"I want to hear about a recent situation that caused you problems,"

I said. "We'll discuss it and then determine where the problems might lie and what changes are needed. I can point out the problems and necessary changes, but it will be your place to make the changes we agree on. How does that sound?"

"Sounds great," Zack said. Connie agreed.

"So tell me about a recent conflict," I said.

Connie started. "This happened yesterday. Zack got upset with me and threatened divorce. He then got so angry he jumped into his truck, slammed the door so hard it hurt my ears, and then sped away. He came back twenty minutes later and tore into me again."

"Oh my," I said, noticing Connie beginning to cry. "That sounds scary. What do you think about what she's saying, Zack?"

"It didn't happen that way at all," he said. "I didn't threaten divorce. I did get into my truck, but I didn't slam the door. I like my truck too much to do that. I left, but then I came back a few minutes later to try to talk things out."

"But you *did* threaten divorce," Connie told him. "You've threatened divorce many times. And you *did* slam your truck door. You also slam the house doors when you're mad."

"Have you threatened divorce before, Zack?" I asked.

"Well, I suppose I have, but I don't remember doing it this time. I might have, but I don't think so."

"So you have other times?"

"Yes."

"And how about slamming doors?"

"Well, I suppose I have slammed a door a time or two. Who hasn't? I'll bet you've slammed a door sometime in your life, haven't you?"

"Zack," I said, "you're not going to change anything you don't own. If you don't own threatening divorce, you're not likely to change that. If you don't own slamming doors, which certainly threatens your wife, you won't change that either."

"Please be honest," Connie said to him. "We want our marriage to be different. You've got to own your anger and what you do and say when you're angry. I know I have things to change too."

"Okay," Zack said sheepishly. "I suppose I have threatened divorce and need to stop that. I need to not get so upset too."

It's no wonder Zack and Connie's relationship is troubled. They have patterns of interacting with emotions that are unmanageable, that must be changed. But they can't change what they don't own. Only when they fully own their problem behavior can they replace it with healthy behavior.

An Effort at Self-Protection

Zack is like many of us, wanting to protect his image of himself. When he looks in the mirror, he sees a man who only occasionally threatens divorce and who closes house and truck doors only firmly. He sees a man who gets upset, not angry.

Unfortunately, unless Zack and Connie look critically at their marriage and name the problems for what they are, they won't experience the healing they seek. Their car (relationship) will continue to run rough, and they won't understand why.

We've discussed the power of denial, which we all use to protect the image we have of ourselves and want to preserve. We ignore our own warning lights. However, when we allow our false, self-protective image to cover the truth, we can't change or grow. Again, we can't change what we don't own.

Change for Zack and Connie began that day with me confronting Zack, time and again, on his minimizing his actions, such as calling his anger simply being "upset." He had to own being capable of scaring his wife when he slammed his truck door, sped out of the driveway, and then came back still angry. He can't change any of these behaviors unless he acknowledges doing them *and* is willing to get to the bottom of why he does them.

This all takes significant work.

To complicate matters, Connie plays a role in all this. She complains about Zack's anger, but she's failed to hold him accountable. She's feared standing up to him and insisting on lasting change.

Change for both Zack and Connie means owning behavior by being truthful about it, feeling sorrow for it, and establishing a clear path for change. Protecting ourselves and completely owning our behavior cannot exist together.

Owning It

Owning our troubled behavior is far more difficult than we might imagine. We all want to explain away our behavior. We want to diminish the severity of it, offering context for why we did what we did. This rarely helps.

Helping people be candid about their efforts at change, truly owning what they're doing and why they're doing it, is a main focus of our work. I offer the following five-step sequence for you to honestly and openly own your bad behavior:

1. *I did it.* Own whatever behavior has been highlighted by your mate. Don't wrap it up in pretty language. Name it for exactly what it is. For example, Zack might say, "I did threaten you with divorce."

2. *It was wrong.* Admit the wrongfulness of your action. Again, Zack might say, "Threatening you with divorce is wrong."

3. *I'm sorry.* If you're sorry, say so. Announce clearly and simply that you're remorseful about the named action.

4. *I can see the impact on you.* This is a validating response, showing you have some understanding about the impact your behavior has on your mate. Zack might say, "I can see that threatening you with divorce erodes your sense of security. It causes you to wonder if I'm committed to you and our marriage."

5. *I would like to do X to make it up to you.* Taking an understanding of the impact of your behavior on your mate as your cue, you offer to "make things right." This

is an act of restoration for damage done. Zack might
say, "I will never threaten divorce again, and in fact, I will
consistently remind you of my commitment to you and
our marriage."

Following and practicing this sequence will bring health and healing to your marriage. You can't change what you don't own, yet what
you own can be felt and understood. In this way you're taking responsibility for "keeping your car tuned."

A Godly Sorrow and Humility

Many couples settle for quick solutions. They won't take the time
or emotional muscle to ask tough questions and press for full ownership. They settle for half-hearted apologies or a quick "I'm sorry" with
little empathy or validation and no clear plan to change.

Real change occurs with sincere remorse and humility. Because the
violator isn't *sincerely sorry*, meaning they haven't grappled with the
full impact their behavior has on themselves or their mate, they won't
really change.

Let me remind you again of my change process with my driving.
Remember Christie complained about it several years previous to me
deciding I needed to change. I had dismissed her complaints, inwardly
believing *she* had the problem. My driving was a problem for her but
not for me.

Only when I felt a godly sorrow, true empathy for her fear of my
driving, did I decide to change. This is true for all of us. As long as
we protect ourselves from the truth (denial), we clothe ourselves with
deception. We remain lost with broken compasses and erroneous maps
and believe the problem is somewhere "out there" instead of "in here."

Let's go back to godly sorrow, this time to what Scripture tells us:
"Godly sorrow brings repentance that leads to salvation and leaves no
regret" (2 Corinthians 7:10). But feeling godly sorrow is no fun. Who
wants to go through the five-step process of naming and owning a
behavior, feeling genuinely sorry, empathizing, and making things

right? This is tough work, but it's the work that brings lasting and powerful change, the work that can make your marriage work.

Get the Most Out of Counseling

Zack and Connie have spent far too much money on counseling. They could have taken numerous cruises and European vacations with the same amount.

I don't say this to be sarcastic or cheeky but to encourage you to be honest with yourself. If you've been to counseling, have you soaked up every last bit of wisdom from the therapist possible, practiced every tool offered, and held yourself accountable for depth change? Have you genuinely felt a godly sorrow that leads to repentance?

I recently read a fascinating article titled "In Treatment: What I Learned from an $800/Hour Couples' Therapist." Jancee Dunn writes that she'd heard Terry Real, "renowned for 'on the brink' one-and-two-day relationship intensives," was a therapist who "took 'tough love' to an entirely new level" and was "shockingly blunt." That turned out to be true for her and her husband—and helpful. Glaring at them, and in no uncertain terms, Real told them things like, "Ridiculing, name calling and lashing out have no place whatsoever in a healthy relationship. There's nothing that harshness does that loving firmness doesn't do better."[17]

I counsel much the same way—in blunt terms—but I'm reminded that so much of what I say to couples has to do with speaking the truth in love, being kind and caring in all that's said. Counseling about that doesn't have to be so difficult and certainly not so expensive. While couples are often well out of practice with this art, their first attempts stilted and difficult, it can be done. They can be motivated to change—and sooner rather than later if they're willing.

Blame Doesn't Work

Keeping your marriage tuned means you give up blame—permanently! Blame is our way of saying "It wasn't my fault," when, in fact, it was.

You're 100 percent responsible for 100 percent of your lane. It's as simple as that. Furthermore, if you'll really own your 100 percent, everything will change.

Why am I talking about blame here? Because it's the opposite of ownership—taking responsibility for keeping our marriage tuned. Blame has two huge problems worth considering:

- *Attributing cause to an event.* A certain event happened *because* of such and such. Often attributing cause to a situation is questionable at best and dangerous at worst.

- *Adding judgment.* Now not only do we create a causal relationship where likely none exists, but we add a moral component—*this is bad.*

When we blame ourselves, we often take more responsibility for a situation than is reasonable. We may inwardly shame ourselves, calling ourselves bad. This plays havoc with our self-confidence and holds us back from challenging the other person to own their part in the problem.

When someone externalizes blame, they refuse to accept responsibility for their role in a problem. Consistently blaming others creates a problem that can't be solved because they believe they've done nothing wrong.

We all know about the blame game. When something goes wrong, someone other than ourselves must be blamed for causing the situation. We stigmatize and judge others, avoiding the five-step process toward ownership I described earlier. Accusing others blinds us and stops us from changing. In the end, blame-shifting hurts others and stops us from growing.

Taking Responsibility for Shortcomings

As we've said, the antidote to blame is taking responsibility for shortcomings. This is no simple task, but it can be practiced and woven effectively into our relationships.

To effectively move into the practice of taking responsibility, you'll have to manage several tasks again and again.

1. *Manage your emotions.* It's difficult—and, in fact, nearly impossible—to avoid blaming when our emotions are running high. We must, therefore, manage our emotions. We must slow down and consider various explanations for why something has happened, being careful not to get bogged down in narrow explanation.

2. *Don't expect life to be fair.* Life is rarely fair, at least in the way we think about it. Bad things happen to "good" people and good things happen to "bad" people. Life is neither fair nor unfair. When we accept this truth, we stop looking to blame others for what happens to us.

3. *Realize you'll never be completely safe in a relationship.* While none of us want bad things to happen to us, we can never be completely safe when we enter into a relationship. It has its share of risks. We may be hurt. We may be betrayed. We may be lied to. While we can do much to guard against these risks, the risks still exist.

4. *Accept that you might never fully explain why something happened.* Most events are multi-causal, and blame/fault-finding attempts to find a simplistic answer to a complex problem don't work. Seeking to explain a complex problem simplistically only causes more problems.

Blame is damaging and must be eliminated from your relationship if you are to have a healthy connection. Be gracious in trying to understand why your mate did what they did, while also holding them accountable yet free from shame. This can be a hard balance to find.

Keep Conflict Simple

In the spirit of keeping your car tuned, let me share some strategies for avoiding costly repairs for your marriage. Ongoing maintenance of your relationship, keeping an eye on the warning lights, is the surest way to avoid costly repairs.

But perhaps the most valuable advice I can offer is to *keep conflict simple*. In other words, handling a situation while it's still small gives you the best chance to resolve it quickly. Pretending a problem doesn't exist (denial) is a sure way for feelings to fester and problems to become aggravated.

Here are five strategies for handling issues simply and effectively:

1. *Stay calm.* Yes, this advice has been cited again and again, but that's because it's perhaps the most effective way to respond to any situation. We think more clearly when all parts of our brain are working, and this is best done with calm.

2. *Agree together on the topic.* From the onset, understand what you're talking about and what you want to accomplish. Knowing the outcome you want helps you formulate what you want to say and how best to say it. Being in agreement with your mate creates an effective connection for solving problems.

3. *Share feelings, not judgments.* We've talked a lot about this. Be *very* careful about blaming, shaming, or judging your mate. You want their cooperation, not their defensiveness. You can do much to navigate this road by sharing from your most vulnerable self.

4. *Respect differences.* You don't need to see things exactly the same. Respect your mate's perspective, show understanding toward it, and seek to help them obtain what they want from the conflict.

5. *Seek collaborative resolution.* Working together, seek solutions you both agree on. Brainstorm answers that meet both of your needs. Remember, if only one of you "wins," you both lose.

I have repeatedly found that finding solutions that work for both parties is often not as hard as we might think. When we keep things simple, paying attention to our process, solutions emerge.

Conflict Containment

There's a time to work on the performance of your engine (your relationship), and there's a time to "put conflict away." A healthy couple has only small islands of conflict and long bridge spans of healthy relating.

Healthy couples also know they must live life amid conflict and that everything doesn't have to be settled *now*. Remember what we learned about *the shift*, about paying close attention to when you're conversing in a healthy way and when you've shifted into your protective, angry, or defensive self. Nothing will be solved if you've shifted. And you *must* remain calm and compassionate, or nothing will get done.

Solomon offers wise counsel: "The prudent see danger and take refuge, but the simple keep going and pay the penalty" (Proverbs 22:3). Seeking refuge may at times mean putting an issue away to be discussed at another time, in another way. The prudent know when a conversation is turning for the worse. Recognizing danger—warning lights—they step aside and call for a time-out.

I teach a tool called Conflict Containment: If after fifteen or twenty minutes you're making no progress at resolving a problem, something is going wrong, and persisting in the conversation is not likely to be helpful. So instead of barreling ahead, set the issue aside for a time. Perhaps you sleep on it. Perhaps you save it for counseling. Perhaps you talk to your pastor about it. For this moment, however, you "containerize" it. You put it in a box and put it on a shelf to be discussed later, at an agreed-upon time and place.

I hear one of you saying, "Great, that's just what my mate wants. To avoid the difficult conversation."

Notice I said to put the issue aside *when you're making no progress*. I also said to agree on a time and place to pick up the issue again, when you're both feeling calm and more compassionate. The issue is not to be avoided but talked about with some emotional balance.

This very well may be easier for one person in a marriage than for the other, but it's a tool all couples must have at their disposal.

Quick Resets

Ideally, you won't need to put an issue aside for long. My hope is that issues are resolved quickly and effectively so you can get on with living life together.

Another powerful tool for keeping your relationship tuned is the *quick reset*. Another term here might be the *do-over*. This requires an ease with which you can say, "I did it. I was wrong. I'm sorry. I can see the impact of my behavior, and I want to make things right with you."

Healthy couples know how to do a quick reset. They don't go hours or days without talking to each other after an altercation. They know this is too painful and causes damage. They know it's better to be connected than to be disconnected, and they will each do their part to own up and get on with it.

A quick reset may mean quickly asking your mate if you can speak to them again, this time more respectfully, about a particular problem. It might sound like this: "I didn't handle the conversation well a while ago, and I'm sorry for speaking harshly to you. I'd like to try again if you're open to that. Might I listen to you again on the matter? I promise to respond better."

A quick reset does not, however, mean simplistic solutions. It doesn't mean I get to harm you and say for the hundredth time, "I'm sorry." That's because a godly sorrow for wrong done leads to repentance—turning away from the wrong behavior.

How do you and your mate do at quickly resetting after a spat? Do you quickly own up, take responsibility, and make things right? Do you look your mate in the eyes and say, "I was wrong. I'm sorry. It won't happen again"?

When woven into a relationship, this tool becomes easier and easier. When you're wrong, you admit it promptly. You've developed your humility muscle and have little need for self-protection. Vulnerability is powerful and effective, and it allows us to do the quick reset.

The Power of Forgiveness

Keeping your car (relationship) finely tuned means you can't harbor bitterness. This is far easier said than done. Who of us hasn't felt bitter toward someone we believed harmed us in some way?

It's our business to keep our hearts clear of bitterness and resentment. No one else can do it for us. We can't wait for others to change their behavior before we'll change ours.

Let's remind ourselves about forgiveness, the challenges of it and the benefits of doing it. Forgiveness is the conscious decision, made over and over again, to let go of negative feelings toward another person. We do this not because that person has apologized (and they may not really be sorry for their actions). We do it because it's the right thing to do.

Most of us believe in the importance of releasing anger, resentment, and hostility. We want to be people who feel compassion and empathy for others. The truth of the matter is this: We won't feel compassion and concern for others as long as we hold resentment toward them. That means the channel between us is clogged with bitterness.

I often find this to be true in marriage counseling. Both parties come to the counseling process saying they want to feel a deep and loving connection to their mate, *but they don't*. What they feel is bitterness and resentment. They have *reasons* for their troubled feelings, citing example after example of how they've been wronged. And they're right! They *have* been wronged.

But now what are they to do? Two people sitting in front of me recount event after event when they've been harmed. Both of their concerns have legitimacy. She can't feel compassion for him because of how he's harmed her. He can't feel compassion for her because of how she's harmed him. We have a standoff.

What *isn't* the solution?

It won't work for them to discuss their grievances at the same time. They've tried this again and again and gotten nowhere. This is called *fighting*. Every couple seeking help has tried either fighting, flighting, or freezing—or some combination of these. They don't work on their problem and only add emotional fuel to the fire.

What, then, *is* the solution?

Forgiveness. Forgiveness isn't sweeping harm under the rug, and it's not some quick fix, a simple "I'm sorry," only to have the harm repeated. Forgiveness involves taking ownership of the ways we've harmed each other, sharing grief and loss together, *with the clear purpose of living life forward.* The question the couple must ask each other is "How can I help you heal so we can ultimately move forward with our lives?" No quick fixes, but no rehearsing wrongs done either. No blame. No shame. Only ownership and a commitment to improve.

Forgiveness comes more easily when both people understand they're capable of hurting the other, even capable of doing to the other exactly what has been done to them. Yet they decide to forgive. Though hurting, they decide to forgive. They make an agreement to live their lives looking forward.

Keep Small Things Small

The easiest way to forgive is to keep small things small. Using our analogy of keeping our car tuned, we will have an easier time of it if we catch a malfunction when it's small.

This is one of the finest pieces of advice my father repeatedly offered when I was facing something difficult: *Is it really that important?*

Of course, this is a simple cliché. When facing adversity, especially if it involves your marriage, the conflict is all you can see. It's all you can think about. It's the most important event on your mind. We all understand because we've all been in a similar situation. However, my father was right. Keep things in perspective. Step back from your situation so you can see the whole picture and other things too.

A problem *feels* huge in the moment, but in time the same problem may well shrink in size. We become more settled with it. We adjust to it and perhaps find a viable solution. Do you trust in your ability to handle whatever comes your way?

Back to my father's advice. Your mate has said something hurtful. Is it really that important? They aren't doing things the way you'd like them done. Is it really that important? Do you really want to make an issue out of this situation?

Cultivating the habit of rolling things over in your mind is a significant tool. It's powerful and takes much practice to exercise effectively. Keeping things in perspective, or keeping small things small, means being able to look at an issue from different perspectives.

One way of keeping small things small is to look at an issue from another person's point of view. For example, how might your best friend describe your situation? How does your mate see a particular problem you're both facing? How might they describe the situation differently from the way you would describe it? These are all different angles from which to view the same event and keep your thinking fluid.

Keeping your relationship tuned means keeping things in perspective. If you use the tools offered in this book, you will grow through your problem, not simply go through it.

And So, What About Love?

Love flourishes when conflict is kept to a minimum and positive regard is reinforced. And this chapter has been about keeping your relationship tuned so you and your mate can journey to wonderful places together. "Keeping tuned" means not allowing conflict to permeate your relationship. You keep conflict in its place by taking responsibility for your shortcomings, keeping conflict simple and efficient. And by forgiving often and remembering we're all doing the best we can.

So love means growing up and facing our weaknesses—we all have them. We admit our weaknesses often and maturely, so problems are kept small. This creates an atmosphere for feelings of love to prosper.

Let's move forward again and explore the power of speaking up.

11

USING YOUR HORN

When You Must Really Speak Up

With regard to navigating relationship's highways and
bi-ways—avoid changing lanes without first giving a signal.

T.F. HODGE

Christie will attest to the fact that a car horn startles me. She's even heard me use "colorful language" when someone around me honks their horn.

Invariably, we'll be driving along when suddenly a loud honk pierces into my consciousness, disrupting my concentration and my peace. I jump to attention, looking around anxiously.

Fortunately, my passenger, Christie, has been observant.

"They're not honking at you," she says reassuringly, knowing I'm inclined to take these honks personally. She smiles at me in her attempt to calm my nerves and reaches for my hand. I nod in recognition, inwardly working on settling my nerves.

In my opinion, a car's horn is the most obnoxious addition on a car. I hate hearing it, and I'm not inclined to use it. I think people use it too often and too insistently. I don't like it.

But to be fair, the horn has an important function—to communicate necessary information. To get attention. It's meant to be heard above other sounds. Have you ever been driving along and drifted into another lane, only to be awakened from daydreaming by the sound of a honking horn? I have, and the sound of that loud horn saved my life.

This chapter is an extension of the last. Sometimes the warning lights we talked about don't get the necessary attention and we need to take the next step to be heard. We'll look at the power of using our bold, blaring horn (our voice and other cues) to offer a warning to our mate or to powerfully reinforce certain behavior. Some people need loud firmness to wake them up. Sometimes a threat of an even greater crisis is needed to alert someone to the need for drastic change. The blaring horn is the proper instrument for these situations, and it's a must tool for a healthy relationship.

Communication—Our Responsibility

Most of us respond positively to a soft request, a gentle voice. Everyday relating largely comprises easy talk, muted gestures, balanced tone inflection, and even volume. Sharing our feelings and needs in a coherent way leads to being understood by others.

Remember, communication is our way of sharing what we're feeling and what we need. This is how we ask for certain behaviors to be repeated, leading to peacefulness and connection. Communication is how we inform others of our desire for certain behaviors to cease, again for the purpose of a peaceful, healthy, interpersonal connection.

Sharing our needs and desires effectively is a powerful and important responsibility. No one can read our mind, nor should they try. We have the power and ability to communicate effectively, offering important feedback to those we care about. While we may become frustrated when others don't understand us, *it's our responsibility to communicate in an effective manner.*

I've emphasized the importance of active listening, paying close attention to what our mate tells us. By active listening, we are attuned to them. We lean in and are sensitive to their concerns. Remember these two critical questions: *What is my mate feeling?* and *What does my mate need?* When we're talking with them, everything they say conveys a need, something we must listen for. Listening and watching for cues is our part in active communication.

While most appreciate gentleness, sometimes raising the intensity and volume of our message, accessing our horn—our strong, clear voice—to share important and critical information is necessary. We're responsible for communicating clearly, effectively, *and sometimes loudly.* If we feel unheard, if our boundaries are violated again and again, we need to ask ourselves whether we've conveyed our message clearly and firmly. Does the intensity need to be turned up to get our message across?

Many people come to me complaining about not feeling heard, blaming their mate for not listening to them. While I'm sympathetic to their frustration, invariably I offer correction. Often it's not the listener missing the mark but the speaker, who's not being as clear and as firm as needed.

I've been working with a young woman who feels very unheard in her marriage. She believes she's communicating clearly, and she doesn't understand why her husband disregards her requests or talks over her.

"If you're not being heard," I said, "it's up to you to speak louder, firmer, and perhaps even stronger."

She didn't like my counsel.

"But I've yelled at him, and he still puts me off. Why isn't it his job to hear me the first time I say something?"

"Yelling is not the same as speaking firmly," I said. "Also, you can't put the responsibility for understanding you on him. I can appreciate you wanting to be heard. I can agree that his behavior is bad. But you must be firm with him. If you aren't, you'll be even more frustrated. Take back your power. Own the task before you, and you'll more likely be heard."

I went on. "The responsibility for being heard is on your shoulders. You are the one who feels the frustration of not being heard, and it's up to you to increase the amplitude, volume, intensity, or frequency of your message."

We've talked at length about speaking clearly and firmly but respectfully to those important to us. With courage, strength, and practice, you will get very good at it. But what if that doesn't work? It may be time to make your message even more powerful.

The Bold Horn

Again, we must know when and how to use our bold horn—our strong, powerful voice. This is no time for subtlety. Subtle cues are hardly noticeable. Sharing indirectly with a glance or a glaring stare, hoping others will pick up our message, fails to convey the seriousness of an issue.

Our message must be bold and clear, powerful and direct. Ongoing complaints and criticism send confusing signals. And criticism spoken in a demeaning way is received differently from constructive criticism spoken with loving firmness.

Using our bold horn, sending a clear, consistent message packed with powerful conviction, is sometimes necessary. When we speak with conviction and boldness, people usually respond.

MaryBeth came to counseling so she could learn to speak up for herself. She's been the victim of emotional abuse for years, and even after separating from her husband, she still suffers from emotional abuse in the form of constant criticism.

"I can't take his criticism anymore," she said, explaining why she separated from her husband. "You don't know how hard it was to leave him. I wonder if I was too harsh with him. I feel guilty."

"Why do you say you were harsh?" I asked. "You've told me you were emotionally abused for a very long time."

"I understand that now. But he doesn't think he's ever mistreated me. Or he calls and promises he'll change."

"Do you see evidence of him changing?"

"No, not really," she said slowly.

"Do you want to go back to him?"

"Oh no," she said, this time responding quickly. "But I feel terrible, and I know I'm sending him mixed messages."

"It took a lot of courage to leave," I said. "I imagine you thought about it a long time before you finally did."

"Yes. I couldn't take his constant criticism and micromanaging my life. I couldn't breathe. I had to get away to think."

"It was a hard decision, MaryBeth, but it sounds like you needed to do it. It was likely the only way your husband would hear you. It often takes a strong message to be heard. A loud, clear message."

I paused to let her think.

"You needed space," I continued, "which is what I hear from many women. You'll know your next step in time."

MaryBeth had a lot of feelings to process. She needed to become comfortable using her strong, bold voice and recognize that using her "horn" protected her. Furthermore, she needed to learn to send cues in a *meaningful* way so they would communicate what she wanted them to convey. Anything less would lead to chaos and the cues not taken seriously.

Merely Noisy Horns

Remember I shared about how I react to horns honking when I'm driving? Now imagine when I'm driving in the city during rush hour, horns blaring, people yelling, and me thinking, *One way. Wrong way. Turn left. No, turn right. Stop. Go. Slow down. Speed up. Pay attention. Relax. Enjoy this experience. Be careful. Danger.*

Yikes! Not only is this my brain when driving in Seattle but it's also my brain when I'm communicating with someone giving mixed messages. Remember, messages are heard when they're clear, concise, and consistent, and now let's add *filled with conviction*. Messages must be coherent, powerful, and meaningful. Anything less is confusing and in danger of sending the following messages, one after the other: *Come close. Get away. I love you. I hate you. I need you. I don't need you at all. I want to be intimate. I never want to be intimate. I appreciate you. I disapprove of you.*

Again, remember the story about Christie complaining about my driving? She inconsistently complained for two or three years before using her bold, strong horn, telling me she would no longer ride with me if I failed to come to a complete stop, use my turn signals, and help her feel safe.

In no way am I placing my irresponsible behavior on her, but had she used her bold, strong voice sooner, I may have taken her more seriously.

You want to be heard and to be taken seriously. You want your mate—and others—to respond effectively to your messages. For this to happen you must eliminate inconsistent messages.

Many couples send inconsistent and even incoherent messages to each other. They each have noisy horns, making complaint after complaint, but they fail to hold their mate accountable for real change. Subsequently, they're not taken seriously.

Noisy horns. Confusing signals.

Since we have a hand on the horn and can control the message we send, it makes sense that we become much more cognizant of this power. *What message am I trying to send? Am I using my horn wisely, effectively? Does the message I'm sending now, in this way, mesh with the other messages I've sent?* You'll know the answer by the results you're getting. If you're sending clear, consistent messages with conviction and accountability, raising the volume when needed, you'll likely be heard.

In a recent counseling session, I met with Gabe and Tanya, who were each hypercritical to the body language of their mate. I was interested in the power of each one's response and reaction to the other.

"Why did you shrug your shoulders?" Tanya asked Gabe.

Obviously startled by her challenging question, Gabe said, "I didn't shrug my shoulders. You're too sensitive."

"Now you're scowling at me."

"Give it a rest," he said, rolling his eyes. "You're really too sensitive."

"You're hurtful, and you just rolled your eyes at me."

And so it went for several minutes. Horns blaring, erratically. No clear, consistent messages. Voices certainly raised. However, neither one was sending a powerful message.

As you consider the above exchange, what do you think? Was she too sensitive? Was he dismissive? Was one of them the culprit and the other innocent?

Other Parts of Our Message

Many of us have experienced encounters like the one with Gabe and Tanya. We've been in a situation where we noticed the roll of the eyes, the frown, the lowered head. We've experienced the condescending tone. These gestures are confusing and add tension to an already tense situation. We must all be aware of how we're using our voice and language to get across the meaning of the message we're trying to convey. We need to learn when to raise our voice to be more emphatic and when to lower our voice for emphasis.

Experts tell us a substantial portion of our communication is nonverbal—through cues. Cues must match our verbal message, or our message gets lost. Let's explore some of these cues. Once we understand them it becomes easier to send clearer messages.

- *Facial expression.* One of the first nonverbal gestures we notice in people is their facial expression. Most of us are aware that a smile tends to elicit a smile and a scowl will elicit a more concerning reaction. How do you typically approach people?

- *Gestures.* We use a variety of gestures when speaking, including waving our fingers or hands, pointing or rolling our eyes. Again, your gestures offer a lot of meaning. Are you aware of the signal you're sending with your gestures?

- *Tone of voice.* Your tone of voice also conveys a lot of meaning. Is it gentle or harsh? Does your tone convey approval or disapproval? A warm tone draws the listener closer while a cold tone pushes them away.

- *Body language/personal space.* Posture and movement convey a lot of information. Sitting a distance from someone suggests distrust or a need for space. Sitting close to your mate, available for touch, conveys openness and receptivity.

- *Eye gaze.* A powerful form of nonverbal communication involves how we look at another person. A harsh glare may be an indication of hostility, while soft eyes suggest interest or attraction.

The central point here is that we send erratic and inconsistent signals all the time, often out of our awareness. The result is confusion. Our mate is unclear about what we're trying to say and what exactly we want to be different. We must ensure that what we're trying to say with our nonverbal communication is in sync with our verbal message.

Congruence

We all want to be heard and understood. This is a primary goal of communication. Using our horn—the volume of our speech and the firmness with which we speak—will either help us be heard or disrupt our being heard. Our horn must be used wisely and be congruent with other aspects of our message.

What do I mean by a congruent message? Congruence is sharing our emotion in such a way that it matches the content of our message. Our strong, powerful voice must mesh with our other communication cues.

This is yet another task that's much more difficult than you might think. Like a horn stuck on or broken and unusable, when emotions aren't shared effectively, we lessen the ability to be heard.

I'm reminded of a woman in her late forties who came for counseling. Susan's nonverbal messaging was malfunctioning, meaning she was sending signals that were hard to interpret. For instance, she continuously smiled as she shared her painful story of abandonment in her marriage.

"Tell me about your marriage," I said during our initial session.

"It's terrible," she said, all while smiling. "My husband is irritable all the time and seems depressed. I try to have compassion for him, but I'm feeling so rejected."

She continued to smile, and she even chuckled at one point.

Initially, I focused on listening to her words, but then I quickly grew distracted when I noticed they didn't match what appeared to be her feelings. I found her body language, tone of voice, and smiles confusing, and I decided it might be important to comment on what I saw.

"Susan, you're talking about very painful situations impacting you greatly. But you're smiling as you tell your story. Are you aware of that?"

"Yes," she said. "I hear that all the time. People are confused by my nervous laughter."

"So you think you laugh out of nervousness?"

"Maybe," she said slowly. "I also know my husband doesn't want to hear me complain, so I stuff my pain when I'm around him."

"So smiling covers your emotional pain?"

"I suppose so," she said, again slowly. She then stopped smiling and began looking down.

"What are you feeling right now?" I asked her.

"I don't know. Upset, I guess. I'm not happy, that's for sure."

"Do you feel sad?"

"I guess so."

"It appears hard for you to give yourself permission to feel what you're feeling."

"My husband doesn't care what I'm feeling. That's why I'm here."

"As important as it is for him to care, and that *is* important," I said, "it's important that you sit with your feelings. It's also important for you to convey a clear, congruent message both to him and to others in your world."

We sat quietly for a moment.

"I'm more aware of your sadness when you don't smile," I said. "There's nothing wrong with smiling, but it's important for your body and presence to be consistent with your words."

I paused to let my words sink in.

"I also wonder if your husband gets confused by your message as well," I said. "I want you to be heard, to be taken seriously, and I want people to know exactly what you're asking for."

This is the point: Our body language, our strong voice—and all the signals we send—must be coherent and consistent with our verbal message. This is how to have the strongest impact.

Inconsistent Messages

Another situation I often find in marriage counseling involves one person sending inconsistent messages to the other.

Jamie is a sixty-five-year-old woman who's been married to Michael for forty years. He's an internal medicine doctor who works a full week at a clinic. They both came to see me because of their increasingly intense conflict.

"He doesn't really care about me or our marriage," Jamie said bluntly during our first session.

"Why do you say that?" I asked.

"I can't count on him for anything. His work always comes first."

I turned to Michael.

"What do you think about what she's saying?"

"It's ridiculous," he snapped. "Of course, I can be counted on. I've been a physician for thirty years, and my patients all trust me. I care for them, and I take my work very seriously."

"But what about your wife and family?"

"They're important to me. I'm just really tired of her complaining. She goes through cycles of complaining, but then everything is fine."

Jamie shrugged her shoulders and rolled her eyes.

"He can't possibly say I haven't been clear," she said to me, then turned to Michael. "I've complained about your work coming first our entire marriage."

"And you've also told me how happy you are for years," he said.

"This is where we reach an impasse," Jamie said, looking to me again. "You hear that I'm unhappy, but he says I'm happy. Help."

Michael responded, "Jamie yells and complains, but she also talks about our nice family and life. Sometimes she's happy, sometimes she's not. I've learned to tune her out when she's down because I know she'll be fine sometime later. I'm never really clear about her concerns."

As I worked with this couple, I found both had legitimate concerns about the other. I *did* find Jamie to be critical and complaining and inconsistent and lacking in specifics when sharing her concerns. I found Michael to be dismissive and distancing. Their messages to each other were hurtful and uneven.

The work I did with Jamie and Michael is work I do with many couples—teaching them to use their strong, bold voices (horns), being crystal clear with expectations, making clear agreements, setting firm boundaries with consequences, and holding each other accountable for change.

Let's look at each of these steps, considering how Jamie and Michael might incorporate them into their relationship.

1. *Be clear with expectations.* We must all think through our expectations of each other. Are they realistic and specific? Are our convictions and values held and spoken firmly? Jamie might inform Michael, "I've been reflecting on changes I'd like to see in our marriage," then say, "Can we sit down and talk about them today?"

2. *Share expectations.* We must share our expectations with our mate. Discussed thoroughly, your expectations become the foundation of trust in your relationship, and ideally, we share them at the beginning of a relationship, though expectations also change over time. Jamie might say, "It would mean a lot to me if we could sit down at the start of the week and make plans for you, me, and our family, knowing I can count on you to follow through."

3. *Make agreements.* Every couple needs to make solid agreements with each other. You'll need to make them about how you'll live, spend money, engage in sex, raise children, and so on. But sometimes an agreement can be simple. Michael could reflect back to Jamie, "I hear you saying you'd like to meet every Sunday evening and talk about the upcoming week. I'm willing to do that."

4. *Set consequences for violated boundaries.* Boundaries without consequences are complaints, and complaints are generally ignored. So couples must discuss their expectations, leading to agreements followed by consequences for violated boundaries. Have you made clear agreements with understood consequences for violations? Jamie might say, "I want our agreements to be strong and clear, where we hold each other accountable for keeping them."

5. *Hold each other accountable.* Agreements are only as good as our power to enforce them. Our power comes from our ability to lean in or lean away in a relationship. Our companionship is the currency we have in our relationship. Holding each other accountable for agreements is an act of dignity. Michael might say, "So we're going to hold each other accountable for keeping agreements. If we fail to live up to an agreement, we need to do something to make amends for our mistake."

6. *Appreciate positive change and ensure a clear message going forward.* It's often not enough to say something once. We must consistently and clearly state our expectations, sometimes more firmly.

Jamie and Michael had much work to do in exploring the values that led to their expectations. At first it was difficult for them to hold each other accountable, to give clear and consistent messages, but they recognized that complaining was not only eroding the positive feelings in their marriage but also sending powerfully negative messages.

Teaching People How to Treat Us

As I watch couples interact and listen to their complaints about not being heard, I often resort to my favorite cliché: "We teach people how to treat us." Think about it. People learn how they can, and must, treat us.

If anyone mistreats us, we're likely not sending a clear, bold message. This is not to justify their mistreatment of us but to emphasize the importance and power of saying something clearly and consistently and then enforcing our boundaries. We must be incredibly clear about what we will tolerate and what we will not tolerate, and sometimes this will involve using our bold horn.

How does this apply to Jamie and Michael? Jamie, as frustrated as she was, had actually taught Michael she could be ignored and dismissed. Now, please don't hear me excusing his behavior. His dismissive and critical attitude and actions were not okay. They were not conducive to a healthy, connected relationship.

But for Michael to change, Jamie had to follow the steps I listed above. She absolutely had to become clear and consistent and utilize consequences. She had to clarify expectations and set boundaries *with consequences.* Could this have led to tension in their marriage? Without a doubt. But the tension would be temporary while they set a new norm for their relationship.

Again, *we teach people how to treat us.* If we reinforce bad behavior by failing to make clear agreements or by failing to follow through with accountability, chaos will result. If the above steps are followed, respect and predictability are the result.

The Bold Horn

Back to the horn—a necessary addition to the car and to our relationships. While I still don't like it, sometimes a strong message must be used. Sometimes we must "lay on the horn," meaning we must speak firmly and forcefully to get someone's attention. At times we must even threaten to pull away from the person or do so for a period of time.

It's our responsibility to speak in such a way that people understand where they stand with us. We must be emphatic, strong, and bold at times to make it clear what we will tolerate and what we will not tolerate.

While we can't force someone to hear us, we can send a strong, clear message, marked by ever-increasing intensity concerning what we feel, think, and must have. We can orchestrate our actions, body language, and words to all come together, forming a powerfully strong message.

Again, it's not just your mate's responsibility to respond effectively, as important as that is. You, the communicator, must also send a strong, clear message.

Here are a few more ideas to practice:

1. *Speak clearly, strongly, and specifically about what you want.*
   Don't expect your mate to read between the lines. It's okay

to be assertive. Christie has said directly and clearly to me, "I prefer to do the dishes. I have a way of doing them I prefer. I'll do them." Boom. Clear.

2. *Share appreciation.* As important as it is to state a preference, it's equally important to positively reinforce that need being met. "Thank you for remembering to put gas in the car after you used it." Wow. I'm going to repeat that behavior!

3. *Share feelings about a situation.* Again, be clear and direct. State a feeling, not an opinion, at least not at first. As you've learned, *a feeling is a feeling, not a thought.* "I feel important when you remember what I've asked you to do and you've agreed to do." Learn the language of feelings.

4. *Listen respectfully.* Yes, we've already dedicated a chapter to listening, but any advice on communication has got to include this: Listen well. Listen actively. "I hear you saying it's important to remember what we've talked about."

5. *Ask questions.* When you don't understand, ask questions. Then continue to ask questions until you're perfectly clear. "I recall you have an event tonight. Can you remind me where you're going?"

6. *Negotiate so both of you feel heard and valued.* It's fine to disagree, but don't stop there. Springboard into negotiating a win-win solution to your problem. "You've shared that you prefer going to our children's house for the holidays. I'd prefer to spend the time home alone. Can we talk about how we can make this work?"

7. *Be firm with what you need.* This is no time to equivocate. Know your limits. Assert yourself. Your mate can't read your mind. "I must be spoken to respectfully for me to listen to you."

8. *Finalize a clear agreement you'll hold your mate to but you're also willing to be held accountable for.* Healthy relationships are built on trust, which is built on agreement. Boundaries without consequences are not boundaries—they're hopes and wishes. Both people must know exactly what they're agreeing to and be willing to be held accountable for what's in the agreement. If in any doubt, discuss the agreement again and write it down. "I believe we agreed to take turns cooking dinner. Is that your understanding too?"

So with good eye contact, body posture facing your mate, and a loving and firm tone, discuss whatever is important to you. But be prepared to increase your intensity to get your point across if necessary.

The Blaring Horn

While I generally recommend communicating with calm, sometimes we must use our horn forcefully—and sometimes really forcefully. Blaring. No one enjoys these experiences, but sometimes raising our voice is important.

Jesus was a perfect example for us. As I read about His time with His disciples, I notice a gentleness in Him. He shared His message in stories, usually with the rapt attention of His followers. The image of Jesus being gentle, kind, and compassionate is woven throughout the New Testament.

Yet a close reading of Scripture shows a Jesus who stood firm and loud in certain situations. Notice His actions with the Pharisees. He cut them no slack and minced no words in communicating His feelings. "Woe to you, teachers of the law and Pharisees, you hypocrites! You are like white-washed tombs, which look beautiful on the outside but on the inside are full of the bones of the dead and everything unclean" (Matthew 23:27).

Here we see Jesus speaking boldly and clearly against a wrong. He wasn't careful with feelings. He didn't follow any of the "rules" I've cited in this book. He was mad over injustice. He was angry at the temple being desecrated. He was repulsed at the haughty arrogance of these phony men.

What is the lesson for us? Sometimes we feel righteous indignation, and so we must stand loudly and firmly against a wrong, consistent but not calm or meek. We must be strong and convey a powerful message: "I'm not happy with this situation. I want change."

A blaring horn can be a message of love.

Music to My Ears

I don't know much about music, but I'm learning. My piano teacher, Claire, teaches me that using soft notes, pianissimo, in combination with crescendos gives the music texture and interest. I'm learning that firm, staccato notes combined with soft, sustained notes make music. Without these distinctions, it's just noise.

As much as I don't like the horn on the car or firm, stern words from my mate, sometimes firmness and sternness—the horn—must be used.

As I listen to Claire play the piano, her exquisite skills mesmerize and inspire me. Those black and white keys can move in harmony, loudness and softness, all working together to make beautiful music.

Our relationship task is similar—to make music. We can use all the tools in this chapter like we use notes on a page of music. Each circumstance has a best tool. Sometimes a soft voice. Sometimes a loud voice. Always a consistent voice. Always a message that conveys meaning to the other. Always speaking from our authenticity.

Picture a symphony. Not only do you see different musical instruments but different musicians with different specialties. Each musician brings something powerful to the full symphonic experience. No sound is extraneous or unnecessary.

And So, What About Love?

While the feeling of love may have been more robust at the start of your relationship, you can still feel very much in love. Your relationship can be vibrant in a new way.

We've discussed the power of communication and how you can positively reinforce people for treating you the way you prefer to be treated. Remember, haphazard actions send an incoherent message, and the listener is apt to be confused. It's up to you to send messages that grow a healthy, loving connection. Sometimes those messages will be soft and warm, at other times firm and bold. Take responsibility for the messages you send to your mate. You have the power and ability to greatly influence your love life. Go for it.

Now let's go to the last chapter, exploring where we've been and how we'll move forward.

12

DRIVING TEST

Putting It All Together for a Love-Filled Journey

Wherever you go becomes a part of you somehow.

ANITA DESAI

My driving history began on a sour note. As a rebellious teenager, I thought I had the right to drive without a license. Citing me for driving without one, Officer Smith disagreed, and Judge Johnson firmly stated I wouldn't be allowed to take my driver's test until three months after my sixteenth birthday.

This really stunk, because I was sure I knew how to drive, and the open road was waiting for me.

My actual driving test was equally challenging. Though I don't remember his name, I do remember the test officer being a stiff and irritable man. I suspect he was aware of my prior citation.

Sitting next to me as I drove, he issued orders.

"Take a left at the light."

I anxiously took a left, swinging into oncoming traffic.

"Get in your lane," he snapped.

Overcorrecting, I hit the curb on the right side.

This was not going well.

"Continue another two blocks and turn right at the light," he said.

As I neared the intersection, the light turned yellow, and I slammed on the brakes.

He looked at me, and I wanted to crawl into a hole. Then he guided me to a place where I could parallel park and told me to do it.

I did, though the car ended up three feet from the curb. He jotted notes about my parking. Then we made some three-point turns and changed lanes, which I apparently did okay with since he was silent.

"Pull in back where we started," he said.

I did that, too, then parked and set the emergency brake. He handed me my test results and said I needed an 80 to pass. Then he got out of the car and walked away.

I gathered enough courage to look at my score. It was 80.

Whew! Who said driving was easy?

Your Driving Test

It's time for your driving test. You've traversed over speed bumps, heeded warning lights, and added trip tips—all in preparation for a successful journey with your mate. You've also learned how to turn a bad trip into a marvelous adventure.

We began our journey together by asking "What's love got to do with it?" When we first chose our mate, most of us believed the feeling of love was enough to create a lasting relationship. But we soon discovered we were wrong. Our old road map or GPS, the one we used for years, wasn't getting us where we needed to go. Faulty thinking, rehearsed and reinforced again and again, led us to faulty guidance.

You're ready for a new direction. It takes more than warm, fuzzy feelings to create a lasting journey, but now you're armed with the instructions you need for a deeper, wonderful journey of love. Putting together all you've learned, you need a review and clear direction before your driving test.

Check Your Baggage

Like GPS that needs updating, emotional baggage must be inspected. Look into your "suitcase" to ensure you've emptied out patterns of behavior and outdated attitudes that distract you from your mission to be the best you can be for the love life you want.

Remember, being only two degrees off can steer you off course. Trusting your old road map and denying being lost just leaves you doing the same old things and getting the same old results. It's time for change. The way you packed for your first journey won't sustain you through the adventures ahead.

Inspect your baggage closely. The emotional bricks in there weigh you down. You need a fresh, new start with fresh, new attitudes and skills. Couples who refuse to explore the depth of their problems struggle.

We can't change what we don't own, and we can't own what we don't see and understand. Denial perpetuates problems. An honest appraisal of your life is the way to pass this driving test. Have you inspected your baggage?

Check in with Your Traveling Companion

Now that you've updated your road map or GPS and inspected your baggage, take a moment to again consider with whom you're traveling. Saying "I do" to your traveling companion once is not enough—choose your mate again and again.

Become more sensitive to your mate's inclinations and preferences. Traveling with someone is vastly different from traveling solo, so be mindful of their thoughts and feelings about the direction you're taking, how you will get there, and your ultimate destination.

The road ahead will have new speed bumps, times when you might question the mate you chose. At these critical times, remind yourself why you chose them. Seeking to cooperate with and complement each other will create an incredible adventure.

Be prepared for issues to arise between you. The adventure wouldn't be exciting if everything down the road was predictable and easy. Instead of recoiling from those issues, embrace them. Embrace your mate and all their idiosyncrasies. These curves and challenges reveal areas needing attention and offer you an opportunity to heal them together. While we all enjoy smooth travels, they don't teach us much.

Choosing your traveling companion again and celebrating this next adventure with them is necessary to pass your driving test.

Beware of the Shift

Beware of "the shift" that signals you're in danger of losing perspective. This shift, when you feel threatened or overwhelmed, is when you're no longer able or willing to stay fully present. When you feel threatened, overwhelmed, and even angry or tempted to withdraw, learn to pay closer attention and make wise decisions.

People in healthy relationships understand these challenging moments happen and use them for growth. Moments of tension lead you to what needs attention, collaboration, and resolution. This will help you pass your driving test as well.

Keep Two Hands on the Wheel

Given the choice of traveling solo or traveling with your mate, the choice is probably easy. Seeing the sights with someone you love, enjoying the adventure together, is often better than being alone.

With two brains focused on the road map, you can journey ahead, working together to solve problems. And with both your hands on the wheel, you can watch where you're going together and recognize the support of your partner. Both people in the relationship must have a voice in where they go and how they get there. With both your hands on the wheel, you and your traveling companion can agree on your direction.

Marriage is fragile, requiring each partner to be mindful of the status of the relationship. Mistakes will be made. Wrong turns will be taken. And that means you-turns and quick repairs are sometimes necessary.

Passing your driver's test requires an awareness of your companion and the deft ability to cooperate with them. Break free from tendencies toward self-centeredness and collaborate with your mate.

Remember, your new motto is "We're in this together, and we can figure it out."

Gain Perspective If You're Driving Alone

Your journey ahead may include times of driving alone. Whatever the reason for this circumstance, it can feel odd, like losing a best friend. And if you've come to rely on your traveling companion, traveling alone may be particularly challenging. The road can seem more perilous.

This challenge is a chance for personal growth. New possibilities emerge with new insights. Take this opportunity to evaluate yourself and your relationship. If there's reconciliation—and I pray there will be—maybe you will ask for more or perhaps you will ask for less.

Make good use of this time and opportunity to drive solo. Rather than focusing on the relationship or your mate, you can focus on yourself. Delve deeply into what you need to learn from this situation. Only when you do this will you be ready to get behind the wheel again.

Mind Any Static on Your Radio

Remember, healthy relating is largely about attunement, tuning your ear to hear what your mate is saying. About listening well.

Most of us live solidly in our own world, thinking self-centered thoughts and doing self-centered things. All the couples we met in this book were in trouble primarily because each person didn't listen well to their mate. Failing to listen, they missed warning signs and grew tragically isolated from each other.

It's time to really tune in. The road ahead will offer many opportunities to listen well to your mate and delight in them. You have the opportunity to learn about what interests them and how their heart beats. Really hear them, noticing both the big things and subtle things.

Create space within yourself to include your mate. Too often we fill our lives with things and our own pursuits, leaving our spouse feeling isolated and alone. To pass your driving test, you must be alert and fully available to them.

Recognize Yellow Lines

As you adventure ahead, become adept at recognizing yellow lines on the road, the demarcation line between where your lane ends and your mate's lane begins.

Drifting into other's people's business is a primary source of relationship conflict. One person falsely believing they're entitled to voice an opinion on matters that don't pertain to them leads to instant conflict. Avoid this. Stay in your own lane. And don't drift into trying to read your mate's mind, telling them how to live their life or judging their actions, thoughts, and feelings. Stay focused on you.

These are particularly difficult habits to break. We often think we know more than our mate on certain subjects. This feeling of self-righteousness leads us to believe we're then entitled to share our thoughts. We're wrong.

Respecting your mate's decisions—unless they impinge on your freedoms—is another form of love. Standing back and biting your tongue when you want to direct your mate's life is a better choice.

Learn to encourage others to manage their own lives, including your mate. Make your boundaries clear, holding them accountable for treating you the way you must be treated. These are required skills needed to pass your driving test.

Stay Focused on Warning Signs

We often drive in an emotional, mental fog and, unfortunately, live in a fog as well. We're rarely intentional about the way we live or the way we relate.

Avoid magical thinking—assuming everything will turn out okay—and become far more alert to danger. Stay focused on the warning lights in your marriage, prepared to slow down, stop, or speed up if they go on.

Danger is all around us, but it can be avoided when you let go of denial—deceiving yourself with wrong beliefs and attitudes. Paying close attention to your feelings and thoughts, you'll be alert to potential problems.

Imminent danger is nearly always preceded by warning signs. As you become more alert to these warnings, becoming more aware of your feelings, you'll make wiser choices enhancing the likelihood of a safe and delightful journey.

As you journey ahead, share your emotions with your mate. Share connecting emotions and be mindful of disconnecting emotions. The way you share your feelings with your mate determines how the conversation will go.

Finally, remember that vulnerability is a fabulous traveling companion. Don't withdraw and protect yourself. Your adventure will be enhanced by being totally available to your mate. Remember, intimacy is *into me see*. Let your mate see into you.

Don't Rely on Just Routine Maintenance

In the journey ahead, make relationship maintenance a part of your life—but not just "routine" maintenance.

Rather, be keenly tuned in to your mate and your relationship. Notice when something begins to go wrong. Be so focused that problems don't catch you by surprise. Catch problems early, when they're still manageable, so solutions are easier. Offer forgiveness.

Understand and accept that significant problems began long ago. Be willing to dive deeply into any problems, discovering and embracing solutions. This work will save you from problems in the future.

This attitude—regular and earnest maintenance—will help you pass your driver's test.

Be Strong in Your Actions

When it comes to setting boundaries and confrontation, sometimes stronger action must be taken. It's your responsibility to set strong enough boundaries so others will respect them. Guarding and enforcing them takes courage and emotional strength.

Sometimes you must be firm, resolute, insistent. And sometimes relationship problems are so bad that an intervention must take place. This is also your responsibility since you teach people what you will tolerate and what you absolutely will not tolerate.

Unclear and inconsistent messages send an unclear message, adding to the problem. Confusing messages become the breeding ground for unhealthy relating.

It's your job to communicate clearly. You've already defined your expectations and boundaries. The final step is holding yourself and your mate accountable for adhering to these expectations. Relationships thrive with clear limits. We thrive with clarity.

Attending to this will ensure passing your driving test.

What's Love Got to Do with It?

Let's face this question one more time: What's love got to do with it?

Feelings of love are wonderful, but you've seen how they can be diminished in many different ways. Emotional baggage, indirect messages, and inadequate attention to your mate's feelings all impact emotional connection.

Feelings of love come and go for various reasons, but fortunately you have the power to ensure they're with you for the majority of your journey. Since feelings of love fluctuate, though, it's critical to maintain a loving attitude and be a loving person. As you cultivate being a loving person, loving attitudes and acts will spontaneously arise out of you. As you tap into skills and mature emotionally, you'll know intuitively how to restore your relationship.

Being emotionally and relationally healthy, the bumps in the road won't unsettle you. The curves and surprises won't be seen as bad, but simply experiences and opportunities.

Consult Your Driver's Manual

It's great to be alive and taking this journey. And you're fortunate to be reading this book, not because it's a great book but because it indicates you're serious about doing the best you can on your trip. And now you've compiled a wonderful set of trip tips—skills—for your marriage journey. You have a driver's manual capable of helping you out of any difficulty in your relationship and pointing you back in the right direction.

Embrace this journey, welcoming challenges as opportunities for growth. Rather than complain about your struggles, see them as windows into your Self and mirrors showing you what needs attention.

Are you ready to pass your driving test so you can move forward in your marriage journey? You can do it. But it takes work and preparation. In our spiritual manual, the Bible, Hebrews 12:1 encourages us to "throw off everything that hinders." Perhaps we can also apply that spiritual truth to our quest for the fulfilling marriage we're striving for, one full of love.

Take the Scenic Route

Last, remember this: When journeying with your partner, you can either take the highway with the same old signs, rigid in your traveling style, or you can take the scenic route with your updated GPS, open to new sights and sounds. Choose the scenic route. Try a whole new path, even if it means risking getting lost. But you've done the work and prepared. You've passed your driver's test. So trust yourself. You can always make you-turns. After all, you're in the driver's seat.

NOTES

1. Richard C. Schwartz, *You Are the One You've Been Waiting For* (Oak Park, IL: Trailheads Publications, 2008), 170.

2. Henry Cloud, *Changes That Heal* (Grand Rapids, MI: Zondervan, 1990), 71.

3. Scott Peck, *The Road Less Traveled* (New York: Simon & Schuster, 1978), 32.

4. Richard Hanson, *Hardwiring Happiness* (New York: Random House, 2013), 12.

5. Anders Carlson, "9 Traits of a Perfect Travel Companion," https://www.orbitz.com/blog/2015/11/traits-of-the-perfect-travel-companion/.

6. Linda and Charlie Bloom, "The Best Preparation for Marriage," *Psychology Today*, May 22, 2017, https://www.psychologytoday.com/us/blog/stronger-the-broken-places/201705/the-best-preparation-marriage.

7. Bloom, "The Best Preparation for Marriage."

8. Tina B. Tessina, "When Love Is Kind: Mutuality in Relationships," https://www.tinatessina.com/when-love-is-kind.html, © 2010 Tina B. Tessina adapted from her books *How to Be a Couple and Still Be Free* and *The Unofficial Guide to Dating Again.*

9. Tessina, "When Love Is Kind: Mutuality in Relationships."

10. "The Mirror Neuron Revolution," *Scientific American*, July 1, 2008, https://www.scientific american.com/article/the-mirror-neuron-revolut/.

11. Brené Brown, *Daring Greatly* (New York: Gotham Books, 2012), 34.

12. Dianne Grande, "Emotional Vulnerability as the Path to Connection," *Psychology Today*, February 24, 2019, https://www.psychologytoday.com/us/blog/in-it-together/201902/emotional-vulnerability-the-path-connection.

13. Kimberly Montgomery, "Signs That You May Need to Set Healthier Boundaries," December 6, 2017, huffpost.com, https://www.huffpost.com/entry/healthy-boundaries_b_9480050.

14. Tamara Thompson, "Talk to Me! 6 Ways to Create Emotional Safety in Your Relationship," January 12, 2018, https://tthompsontherapy.blog/2018/01/12/talk-to-me-6-ways-to-create-emotional-safety-in-your-relationship/.

15. Marshall Rosenberg, *Nonviolent Communication* (Encinitas, CA: Puddledancer Press, 2015), 41.

16. Rosenberg, *Nonviolent Communication*, 41.

17. Jancee Dunn, "In Treatment: What I Learned from an $800/Hour Couples' Therapist," *The Riveter*, https://theriveter.co/voice/lessons-from-couples-therapy/.

ABOUT THE AUTHOR

With more than 30 years of counseling experience, **David Hawkins,** PhD, has a special interest in helping individuals and couples strengthen their relationships. Dr. Hawkins's books, including *When Pleasing Others Is Hurting You, Dealing with the CrazyMakers in Your Life, In Sickness and in Health,* and *When Loving Him Is Hurting You* have more than 500,000 copies in print.

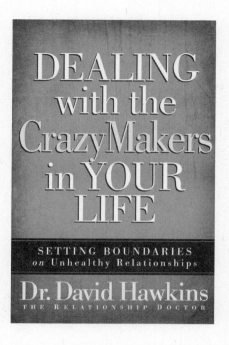

Dealing with the CrazyMakers in Your Life

Some of the most difficult people to deal with are those who fail to take responsibility for their lives and who wreak havoc in their relationships. Author and relationship doctor David Hawkins offers help for those caught unavoidably in the craziness of a disordered person's life. With clear explanations, examples, and real-life solutions, Hawkins shows readers

- how to develop healthy life skill tools and boundaries,

- when, why, and how to confront a person who drives them crazy, and

- how disordered people think, act, and see the world

Anyone trapped in another person's cycle of disorder will discover ways to change their own response, perspective, and communication—and ultimately find the hope of peace in the chaos.

When Pleasing Others Is Hurting You

You want to do the right thing—to take care of your family, to be a good employee, to "be there" for your friends. And you're good at it. Everyone knows they can depend on you—so they do.

But are you really doing what's best for them? And what about you? Are you growing? Are you happy and relaxed? Are you excited about your gifts and your calling? Or do you sometimes think, "I don't even know what I want anymore."

Find out why you have trouble saying no. Learn why you feel accepted only when you are producing. And finally experience the deep joy and peace that come with serving other people out of your abundance, not out of your need.

To learn more about Harvest House books and
to read sample chapters, visit our website:

www.harvesthousepublishers.com

HARVEST HOUSE PUBLISHERS
EUGENE, OREGON